THE BREAD IS IN THE BED

How to Make More Money as a B&B Innkeeper

By Glen and Ann Stanford

THE
BREAD
IS IN THE
BED

How to Make MORE Money as a B&B Innkeeper

By Glen and Ann Stanford

Copyright

The Bread is in The Bed

How to Make More Money as a B&B Innkeeper.

Copyright © 2013 by Glen and Ann Stanford

Cover illustration by John Cole; inquiries regarding John's illustration and cartoon work can be made via h20vale@msn.com.

Published by Stanford & Stanford Publishing, Naples, Florida

ISBN: 978-0-9889819-3-5

In Memory of

Fellow innkeepers gone but never forgotten:

Cheryl

Kirsten

Margaret

Patrick

Richard

Disclaimer

Neither the authors nor the publisher assume any responsibility or liability whatsoever on behalf of the purchaser or reader of these materials. Any perceived slight of any individual or organization is purely unintentional. The publisher and the authors make no representations or warranties with respect to the accuracy or completeness of the contents of this work and specifically disclaim all warranties including without limitation warranties of fitness for a particular purpose. No warranty may be created or extended by sales or promotional materials. The advice and strategies contained herein may not be suitable for every situation. This work is sold with the understanding that the authors or publisher is not engaged in rendering legal, accounting or other professional services. If professional assistance is required, the services of a competent professional person should be sought. Neither the publisher nor the authors shall be liable for damages arising hear from. The fact that an organization or website is referred to in this work a potential source of further information or as a citation and does not mean that the author or the publisher endorses the information the organization or website may provide or recommendations that it may make. Furthermore, readers should be aware that internet websites listed in this work may have changed or disappeared between when this work was written and when it is read. While all attempts have been made to verify the information provided in this publication, neither the author nor the publisher assumes any responsibility for errors, omissions, or contrary interpretations of the subject matter herein. This book is for entertainment purposes only. The views expressed are those of the authors alone, and should not be taken as expert instruction or commands. The reader is responsible for his or her own actions. Names have been changed as needed.

Table of Contents:

Introduction

This book is the layered onion of e-books, but less stinky.

On the outside it's a humor book that will bring tears to your eyes; and inside of that it's a business book; and inside of that is some sage advice on customer service; and deep down inside of that is the one-of-a-kind advice specifically tailored to the innkeeper on how to make money today, tomorrow, and in the years happily ever after.

YES! There is a way to make money as an innkeeper! This book cuts to the most important aspect of innkeeping: profit! What? Isn't the lifestyle the most important? Isn't it the joy of owning your own business? Isn't it the pride in one's soul that can only be achieved with a clean, shining toilet?

Maybe so, but if you don't have the money to keep your dream going, you'll never get a chance to take pleasure in your new career. This book addresses (what should be) your biggest fear: "How do I get money into the cash register?" You can work on your fear of napkin folding on your own time.

THE BREAD IS IN THE BED might not be a humor book in the strictest sense. It's more the literary equivalent of a genetic love child from Leona Helmsley, Dave Barry, Dale Carnegie and Donald Trump. You'll learn valuable secrets to making (more) money in the innkeeping business, all the while keeping your sense of humor, winning friends, influencing people, and maintaining epic hair. It's a funny book, it's a business book, it's got unique innkeeper advice, it's a breath mint and it's a candy mint!

"Ah ha," you say, "Jack of all trades, master of none." Guilty as charged. But let's modify that expression to "Jack of all trades and decidedly good advice on one – the innkeeping money stuff!" And despite all the discussion about the innkeeper's cash register, this is a fun book that will make you smile, *particularly* if you have no intention of ever owning an inn!

Nowadays, entrepreneurship is the widest highway to financial success. There is risk and reward in every job, but you only have so much time to devote to your occupation. If you want to quit the rat race and run your own rats, you need to become an entrepreneur. If you want your inn, B&B or guesthouse to actually make money, this could be a pretty important book in your arsenal.

After 27 years (and counting) as entrepreneurs, we believe that running your own business is the surest way for most people to maximize the reward of their efforts. We're going to help you find the best location for your new property, giving you some useful advice before it's too late. Then we'll talk about how an attitude adjustment can lead to increased profits.

Sure, it can be scary to strike out on your own. Maybe that is why innkeeping attracted me in the first place. I knew that I already had many of the skills required to keep an inn. I could flip a pancake, make a bed (occasionally) and pour a beer (more than occasionally). What else did I need to know? Ahh, the ignorance of bliss, I remember it well.

(One odd convention you will encounter throughout the book is the switching between first-person singular and first-person plural. When you encounter the word "I" it means that Glen is telling a story and trying to be funny, and Ann has disavowed all knowledge, like the recording at the beginning of every *Mission Impossible* episode. So, I'm the "I" and Ann and I are the royal "we." Why am "I" not surprised?)

We're going to tell the innkeepers out there how to make more money starting today! And we really mean *today* (if you have guests in the inn tonight, that is.) Then we're going to tell you the things that you can do to make more money *this month*. And then, most importantly, we will outline the strategies that you can begin to use starting immediately that will improve your profitability *this year* and in *every year* to come.

There's a big hint on how you are going to do this right on the cover of this book: the bread is in the bed! The money is in the mattress! The profit is in the pillows! You won't be making your big profits by selling golf shirts, souvenirs, or even meals and drinks. Your laser focus will be, must be, putting heads on the pillows.

Running a Bed and Breakfast for Dummies by Mary White is a tremendous compilation for _every detail_ you might need to consider before purchasing a hospitality property, and we highly recommend it. For better or worse, our book is _much_ more streamlined and opinionated (and the humor is spicier!) We're going to tell you the best ways that _we_ have found to succeed in this business, and 15 years of pancake flipping and bathroom cleaning confers a certain amount of street cred.

You might as well go get a whole bucket of asterisks because there are many ways to skin the innkeeping cat, and you will likely take issue with some of our opinions. The smart reader will understand that we don't mean to sound like know-it-alls, but we do have some interesting things to say. Then again, if you were smart, you wouldn't be getting into the innkeeping business, now would you?

Think of us as little imps sitting on your shoulder as you are reading the traditional "How to be an innkeeper" type book, smacking you upside the head and saying "pay attention here, this is important, this is the good stuff."

Once you buy your inn, you are automatically enrolled in the school of hard knocks. It is our intention to help you earn enough money to pay your tuition and graduate. We genuinely believe in what we're trying to convey: Innkeepers can absolutely make more money without having to go through (too much of) the painful learning curve.

The last section of this book is "War Stories from Innkeeping Hell." Most are comical, some are incredible, and most of them should help to talk you out of ever buying a country inn!

You'll find some stories that illustrate why you need to have an emergency fund for a rainy day. We will talk about where you should spend money and when you should keep it in your pocket. You've got to, as Kenny Rogers sings, *"Know when to hold 'em, know when to fold 'em."* Bruce, who runs the Inn at Water's Edge in Ludlow, Vermont with his lovely wife Tina, once gave me this excellent advice: "never trade with scared money." I told him that all my money is petrified, thank you very much.

You will need an emergency fund for the unexpected things that seem to happen only to innkeepers (what's up with *that*, anyway?) Let's say - to choose an illustration completely out of thin air - that a deer jumps through your back window and rampages through your downstairs. Yes, that happened to us (and more on this incident later). I looked everywhere in the budget for "deer rampages" but couldn't find a thing.

Although it is on its surface a humor book, I'm the first to admit that it's not in the league with Dave Barry (my hero). His books will give you a laugh in every line. Well, maybe not every line, let's call it three laughs and a chuckle in every paragraph. On average. Okay, sometimes there's a guffaw thrown in for good measure. I think that ideas that go into our brain with emotion tend to be memorable, so I'll try to shoehorn the good stuff into your cranium with a funny bone.

Although it's not a customer service book, we'll tell you some critical things to work on that will help you in the real innkeeping world. We recommend Dale Carnegie's *How to Win Friends and Influence People*. It's a 1937 classic that has withstood the test of time.

This is not a comprehensive book on innkeeping; we focus on a few key items that will increase your profits as an innkeeper. I'm not going to give you toilet paper folding or flower arranging advice, nor will I tell you how to write a business plan. Don't get me wrong; these are all good things, but they just won't help you put money directly in the till.

Even the business plan part. Whenever we need a good chuckle, we go back and read our original, tidy business plan. Boy, were we green! Many of the things that we thought would be important (and the banker agreed were important) turned out to not be the things that actually put cash and coin in the drawer. Don't get us wrong, it was an excellent business plan as business plans go: the i's were dotted, the t's were crossed, and phony baloney estimations were made.

Most innkeeping books will lay out your many options. They'll tell you to do a business plan; do your market research. No offense, but umm, *duh*. Now that you've done that market research and written that business plan, does it make sense in the real world? This book takes it that last crucial step - we give you *opinions*, not just *options*.

We're also going to tell you *why you should not become an innkeeper*. Okay, I've said it – this is really the biggest hint in the book to help you save money – *don't buy an inn!* But if you *are* going to do it, then do it right.

Some innkeeping books do their duty and have that cautionary paragraph where they tell you: yes, it has long hours; yes, it is hard work; and yes, it takes a special kind of person to be an innkeeper. These admonitions that only hint at the warnings are much too brief in our opinion, and we're going to spend some time trying to talk you folks out of it! Okay, we'll tell a few nice stories too, but if your spouse is trying to convince you to buy a country inn and you think it's a crazy idea, point him or her toward the *War Stories from Innkeeping Hell* chapter.

This book is laid out in two parts: BEFORE you buy your inn and AFTER you buy your inn. You will benefit the most from this book if you haven't pulled the trigger just yet and are still looking for your property. If you are in the business, all is not hopeless (though it just might seem that way).

If you bought the book after you have decided to buy a specific inn (or, heaven forbid, already own one) you might feel slightly disappointed because a good chunk of this book is devoted to *War Stories* that might talk sensible folks out of an innkeeping career. If I were you, fellow innkeeper, I'd go grab a beer and read that section anyway. You'll get a chuckle or two and nod your head through it thinking "I believe *that* one." In any event, you can reread it when you're totally burned out and need to know that others have felt your pain.

Let's agree that there will always be exceptions to the advice in this book. I would run out of ink putting asterisks throughout this book if I was making the claim that I have the ultimate answer to Life, the Universe, and Everything (which we all know is "*42*," as we learned in <u>The Hitchhiker's Guide to the Galaxy</u>). This guidance is suitable for most of the people, most of the time, and I'll leave it at that. Then again, what are you expecting from a book that you can buy with the change you found in your sofa?

Every innkeeper out there could write a how-to book on the nuts and bolts of innkeeping. It's important information to know, and the sooner you know it the better. We joke about things like napkin folding and towel origami, but these are skills that you'll develop and will be useful in your work. You'll also need to work on your cooking skills, maintenance skills, record-keeping skills, cleaning skills, decorating skills and commode shining skills. But never lose sight of the *most effective skills* that add up to putting money into the cash register – sales, customer service and marketing.

Hidden inside the humor are innkeeping nuggets that you can use *from this moment forward* to make your bank account grow. Some stories might seem wacky and bizarre, but that is only because innkeeping *is* wacky and bizarre!

If you already are an innkeeper, we promise that you will hear something new in this book. I can sense you rolling your eyes now. You've seen it all. We know you are a tough crowd to please. We innkeepers tend to get quite opinionated (and some of us are occasionally known to keep it to ourselves).

It is likely that if you're already in the biz that you *already* know the advice in *most* of these sections. You can skip to the ones that are new concepts. As an added bonus, you will not have to slog through all of my alleged humor.

PART I – BEFORE YOU BUY

The Gleam in Your Eye

If you have not purchased your hospitality property yet, it is not too late to maximize your chance for success. There are quite a few things that you can still do to lay a better foundation for a successful business.

The tastiest morsel of this book might be the discussion of three critical items that will give you the best chance to succeed (other than a winning lottery ticket): Location, Food and the "It" factor. If you can hit home runs in these categories, you will lay the foundation for a rock-solid business. (If you can hit *real* home runs, please apply at Fenway Park.)

Here's a little hint: *every inn is for sale*. Every innkeeper is burnt-out to some extent and would consider selling at the right price. If you find a property that you like, then go inside and look around. If you see more than a half-dozen hand written signs telling you not to clip your toenails in the common areas or not to put baby powder on the dog, then the innkeeper is *just* a little burned out.

When Don and Ginny sold us their inn, it was not *technically* on the market. We loved the look of the inn, knocked on their door and asked if they would ever consider selling it. Looking back we have to laugh at ourselves. Of course they had considered selling, they were innkeepers!

Don't limit yourself to inns that a real estate agent is going to show you or what you find in the MLS. While you can still get valuable information from brokerage sales packages, these are not your only choices, or even your best choices.

LOCATION Cubed

Area Draw

"Hey, you said that there wouldn't be any math!" Okay, make that *location, location, location*: the three most important real estate considerations.

You want to be near a tourist draw, not just a stopover for someone passing through. You want to be a destination inn, not a one night stand.

As a general rule, if there are a few inns in the area, then there is enough tourism to support another one. We're not saying that you should build one, but you should look for towns with multiple hospitality properties. *"If you are the only, then you'll only be lonely."* (I'm a poet and I don't know it; but my toes show it, they're Longfellows.)

There are pockets of innkeeping prosperity that have put themselves on the map. Cape May, New Jersey has developed a fine reputation for small lodging properties. Look for these pockets of prosperity where the market research has already been done.

When I was growing up in the Chicago area, there was a management school for a fast-food chain that was building restaurants all over the country. But before they allowed their franchisees to build a restaurant just anywhere, they required an in-depth study of the traffic and customer demographics. They wanted every one of their franchisees to succeed, and were (at the time) very strict about where you were allowed to put a restaurant. You may have heard of this company; it's called McDonald's and they sell a lot of hamburgers.

There was another company that also had a pretty good business idea. When golden arches were planted in the ground, this company would buy the lot across the street and put in a hamburger joint of their own. This company was called Burger King, and they did pretty well, too. So learn from the King, let someone else do the market research for you! If there are a few prosperous inns in the area, then one of them is probably a reasonable choice to consider purchasing. If there are *fifteen* prosperous inns in the immediate area, now you're cooking with gas!

What is the draw to the area? Is it a ski resort, an amusement park, a golf resort, or is it just a "really nice area?" There's nothing necessarily wrong with a "really nice area," but we would like it better if you can fill in the following sentence: guests will come to my door because we are right next to "blank," where "blank" is a place that *many people* like to visit every year.

Road Appeal

Sun Tzu said in the _Art of War_ that "every battle is won or lost before it is ever fought." I'm pretty sure that Mr. Tzu was an innkeeper, and that he was talking about _road appeal_. Set yourself up for success by purchasing a property with _road appeal_. Walk-in guests are important and you want to get the traveler to slow down and poke his nose in your front door. (Well, not actually _bumping into_ the front door. That might hurt. Him. Not the door.)

We'll admit that beauty is in the eye of the beholder (beer holder?) and we thought that _our_ inn looked quite pleasing. We tried not to be _too_ insulted when a guest would say, _"This place looks so much nicer on the inside than I thought it would."_ We heard it enough times to realize that there was probably some truth to it. Hordes of people must have passed us by over the years because we did not look as inviting on the outside as we were on the inside. This led to a major renovation in the front yard and the installation of a 100-yard long garden in an effort to improve the view from the highway.

We understand that _road appeal_ is subjective, but try to remember the details of your _first impression_ when you visit properties. I think that Mr. Tzu was also the guy who said "never kick a fresh turd on a hot day," so you can be sure that this dude knew what he was talking about.

Bullet Dodged

One inn that we looked at was in the lovely little mountain town of Rochester, Vermont. We were living in the Boston area at the time and didn't have too much of an idea about the inn business other than we knew (or at least foolishly thought we knew) that we wanted to be a part of it.

We found an absolutely gorgeous property that was up and running as an inn and restaurant. When we visited with the broker, we learned that they were doing most of their business serving lunch to the locals. (We were also told not to pay attention to the smashed plasterboard in the men's bathroom. It was just a small misunderstanding between a couple of loggers, and the wall would be patched before we took possession.)

We thought that this place was wonderful despite the stories of the occasional fisticuffs. Here we had a built-in restaurant business, complete with a very impressive commercial kitchen. There were 20-something bedrooms just waiting to house eager skiers. The inn was "conveniently" located halfway between Killington and Stowe ski resorts, the two most popular in the state, on the same road only 1 ½ hours away in either direction! You could have stayed with us and decided each day what resort you wanted to visit; what could be wrong with that plan?

Boy, did we dodge a bullet (or two) in not buying that property. It would have violated two of the important guidelines in this book: (1) location cubed and (2) bar business scares away room business (*THE BREAD IS IN THE BED*, not in the pub.) Buying an architecturally striking property was tempting, but while this inn was strategically located between the two biggest ski resorts in the state, it was not actually *close* to either one of them. If we were lucky, we might get a traveler just passing through, but there is *no way* that a skier would spend three hours commuting back and forth to the slopes every day just to stay with us.

The last time we looked, this facility had been turned into a retirement home, which makes a lot of sense. It is now probably being operated in its "highest and best use," a term that appraisers are fond of using. It would have been a multi-million dollar property if it could have been airlifted and dropped right next to a ski area, but in the middle of nowhere it was just a big beautiful white elephant.

Our Miscalculation

The inn that we eventually bought was in Plymouth, Vermont where Calvin Coolidge was born (the only President born on Independence Day – go win a bar bet today.) Silent Cal was also raised, inaugurated and buried there. The most interesting fact, in my opinion, was that he was *inaugurated* in our tiny town (Pop. 400). President Harding died in office in 1923, and VP Calvin was back at home when the call came from Washington. Cal's father, a Justice of the Peace, administered the Presidential oath of office by candlelight that night. Quite a contrast to today's dog and pony shows, wouldn't you say?

We became the proud new owners of the Salt Ash Inn in Plymouth, Vermont, home of the Calvin Coolidge Homestead, the fourth-most popular tourist attraction in the state. One would have thought that it was a no-brainer that we would get gazillions of guests from this well-known attraction. We never stopped trying to milk this cow, but alas, she was dry. Eventually your arms just get tired and the cow gets pissed off.

The best illustration of our miscalculation was made clear to us on July 4, 1987 on what would have been Coolidge's 115th birthday. There was a special event at the Homestead that had been advertised around New England for quite a while, and big crowds were expected. As new innkeepers, we were doing everything that we could to try to make ends meet, so we opened the restaurant to the public. We had sandwich board signs out front and local advertising to try to corral some of the drive-by traffic going to the Homestead.

I got out our huge 15-gallon beer brewing pot and made a batch of chili in the back yard (and I looked comical stirring it with a canoe paddle). Of the thousands of people who visited the Homestead that weekend, we hosted exactly one overnight room and maybe a couple of dozen lunch goers. We did have very delicious left over chili for the next year and a half.

So can you guess what our problem was with the Calvin Coolidge Homestead? While historic and quite interesting, *it takes only about an hour to visit!* If you drag your feet, stop at the Plymouth Cheese Factory, read every exhibit, stroll through the aisles of the re-created general store, then maybe you can extend your stay another hour or so. The point is people didn't come to the Homestead requiring overnight lodging – they certainly were not going to spend *two days* at the Homestead.

Fortunately for us, and the main reason we bought the inn, was that one of the several entrances to the largest ski resort on the East Coast (Killington) was located only 5 miles up the road. The nearly 5-mile long access road to the Killington base lodge was only 30 years old, so there were no 19th century country inns on it. There were plenty of nice lodges and motels, but no historic lodging properties.

If a skier wanted to ski Killington and stay at an historic country inn, we were the closest to the slopes. That tiny sliver of a big pie allowed us to fill all our weekends from mid-December until mid-March every year (and we could have filled them twice over). Our mid-week occupancy was all over the lot, but always filled on the holiday weeks. The season average was about half filled for mid-weeks. This was pretty typical of the area, and we expect that most innkeepers in ski country would tell you the same.

Are you beginning to see the difference between the two draws? You need to have a property where people can stay for *more than one night* to enjoy the activities in the area! Now is the time to find a place like that. Look for a place where guests will stay with you for multiple days, either for a weekend or (even better) for week-long stays. There is a reason that inns on the New Jersey shoreline have developed a fine business. It is traditional to take week-long summer vacations at the beach!

There are a few things that you can do to compensate for a less than ideal location, and we'll talk a little about them later. Sometimes you'll need to string several events and activities together to keep full. While a festival, fair or special event might help to boost your business, strong profits can't be built around one-time events. You need a steady draw that will keep people overnight for days at a time. Things like amusement parks, ski areas, and even large museums will keep travelers under your roof for multi-day stays.

FOOD – Hunger Pains

This may come as a shocker, but a lot of people like to eat dinner every single day!

Are restaurants located <u>very</u> conveniently to the property? If not, do you intend to offer (at least) two meals a day? You can probably get away with not serving lunch, and even going easy on the morning meal by serving a "hearty continental" breakfast. But the evening meal is another matter, and if it is difficult for your overnight guests to find a convenient dinner, you will be fighting an uphill battle for your whole innkeeping career.

The best location will be one where your guests can walk to dinner. It can be either downstairs to your dining room or across the street to another restaurant or two. There are compromises that you can make to improve a less than ideal situation, but if you are really starting from square one, look for convenient access to food. Delicious and affordable food would be a bonus!

IT is Very Nebulous

In a famous 1964 obscenity court case, Justice Potter wrote that while *he might not be able to define pornography, he knew it when he saw it!* Your property should be just as remarkable, if not as scantily clad.

It's challenging to make a checklist that will tell you if a property has the "It" factor: the vital quality *of the facility* that allows a guest to relax and be comfortable. You will be adding the personal touch, but the buildings and grounds must do their part as well.

Visiting multiple Inns, Bed and Breakfasts and Guesthouses will help you get a sense of what works and who has "It." Keep "It" near the top of your checklist of items to look for, even if it's a vague element.

Use George W's fuzzy math and rate it on a scale of 1 to 10. Ask other overnight guests what they think about the property. What were *their* first impressions?

Have your friends stay in the properties that make your short list, and ask them about their first impressions. If you go with them, you'll see how well the property allows groups of people to feel comfortable together.

You want to have a property like this because you want to book blocks of rooms and host groups of guests. It is a heck of a lot easier to fill blocks of rooms than to have to fill the units one at a time. We would estimate that 80%

of our weekend rooms were taken by groups or at least big blocks of people who knew each other.

When you walk into the property, do you feel *instantly* at ease? Does your jaw drop at how wonderful the place is? Can you imagine yourself as a guest here? Your first impression is *huge* because that is the foundation of your guests' experience.

If you walk into a property and think *"Oh, it's nice enough, but if we make such and such a change we can make it look more inviting,"* then we urge you to walk away. You may indeed improve it, but chances are the property does not have the nebulous "It" factor.

WHAT KIND of Property Should I Buy?

Do you want a bed and breakfast or an inn? What's the difference, anyway? Do you want a guesthouse, a strip motel, or do you want to open a couple of spare bedrooms to take in some money on the side?

You might be surprised, but we have very definite opinions here! Most books are going to give you all of the options and let you decide which one best suits you. We're going to tell you the one that best suits your bank account.

First, let's discuss the difference between a bed-and-breakfast and an inn. There is no official distinction of which we are aware. In fact, there are quite a lot of big motel chains that like to staple the word "Inn" to their name, presumably because it makes them sound quaint. Inns are personal, homey, and comfortable. They are everything that the big box motels want you to think about when you think of them: Holiday, Red Roof, and Comfort come to mind.

Visiting a B&B is more like going to someone's home where they have many bedrooms and not much in the way of common areas. There might be a small sitting room, but for the most part you feel like you are visiting Aunt Mabel who makes great waffles.

A country inn will have *larger common areas* where you are likely to meet other guests. The room where you park it to eat the waffles will be larger, and will look more like a restaurant than auntie's dining room. There is probably a bar area or at least a recreational room with games and a lot of seating.

A Guest House is somewhere between the two, but if we can't describe the difference off the top of our heads after fifteen years in the biz, then you can be sure that the traveling public is just as perplexed. A strip motel is an entirely different business, and although it may be the same size, there is very little interaction with the guests. Spare bedrooms are just that, a couple extra beds down the hall in your home, and while a few of these techniques still apply, lodging won't be a stand-alone business for you.

Here is where we would run out of ink with all of the asterisks. Of course these are generalizations! We are just clarifying the terminology of the industry so that we can communicate on common ground. Now put your hand down and pay attention with the rest of the class.

Let's agree that a Country Inn is generally larger than a Bed and Breakfast. It's similar to the old Navy expression explaining the size difference between a boat and a ship: a boat will fit on a ship, but a ship won't fit on a boat.

We understood the confusion in the eyes of the public, and that is why we called ourselves *both* a B&B *and* a Country Inn in our advertising and on our signage. However you classify your property, the key to success is having *the large common areas where guests can relax and mingle.* These are more likely to be found in a country inn.

<u>In our opinion, using the definition above, you are more likely to succeed if you own a country inn.</u> Otherwise, it will be difficult to capture the group business and you will miss out on a big profit center. You need to have obvious and convenient areas for two dozen or so people to gather and enjoy themselves without feeling like they're bothering a homeowner.

Size Matters

Unless you are in a 365-day tourist area, like somewhere in Hawaii or possibly next door to a large *popular* year-round amusement park (with mouse ears, maybe), there are practical reasons that you will need a minimum number of rooms to pay the bills.

The old industry standard was that you required a minimum of eight rooms to make it in the business. We think that eight rooms could be a struggle for many people, and that you should look for properties larger than that. Sometimes guests will work their traveling schedule around you, but more often you'll find that if you can't accommodate them on a certain night they will move on to the next property.

There will be plenty of slow days when you only have a few rooms filled, so you need to have the capacity to make lots of hay when the sun is shining and the area is full of tourists. We would strongly urge you to look for a property with twelve or more bedrooms to give you the best chance at success. There are plenty of smaller inns doing quite well, we know, but these are special cases.

The average size inn in our innkeeper association (approximately 20 inns) was around a dozen rooms; we were one of the larger ones with eighteen bedrooms (by the time we sold in 2001). The smaller properties tended to struggle because if you can fill eight rooms, you can fill twelve (and if you can fill twelve, you can usually fill eighteen). So on the days that things were busy, everybody did well, but the larger places did *very* well; on the days that things were slow, everyone in town was slow with only a few rooms.

Of course more bedrooms are going to cost you more money. Everything is a trade-off. Looking back, we would probably have preferred a 10-room property with no mortgage to an 18-room property with a big mortgage. The happy medium is somewhere in between and will be different for everyone.

As a quick aside, don't forget to be flexible by allowing guests to sardine themselves into a single room. Have *day beds* (instead of twins or a sofa bed) with trundle beds under them. Also, have a half-dozen twin mattresses (on or off cot frames) available in a closet. Often this makes the difference when it comes to booking a room. When you tell a family of four that the last room left only has a queen bed in it, but that you'll be happy to make-up twins on the floor for the kids, they'll thank you for your trouble (and the kids will think it's an *adventure* like camping). In any case, *it's the guests' decision* and you benefit from the "extra person" charges as well. Repeat after me, *THE BREAD IS IN THE BED.*

While we're on the subject of adventure, I once told Ann that sleeping on a boat would be "just like camping." She said, "*Yeah, right. Like camping in a washing machine.*" Women.

Once we had a guest who told us at check-in that we would need to charge her for an "extra person" because her Great Aunt was with her. We asked if she needed a cot, and laughed when she said, "No, she's in an urn."

New or Used?

Should I start my inn from scratch, or should I buy an existing business (and probably pay more)? If you build it, will they come? It worked for Kevin Costner in the *Field of Dreams*.

But it won't work for you. Do not, we repeat, do not even consider starting an inn from scratch. Now there's a timesaver! Jump right to the next chapter if you're on the speed reading plan; you won't miss a thing.

We can appreciate the temptation to try to save a little money by starting your business from scratch. Or maybe you want to design the inn *exactly* to your specifications. There are a few success stories that attest to the fact that it *can* be done. We are going to tell you now, *don't do it!* Odds are that you will create a fine property that will be incredibly inviting, and the innkeeper who buys it at your bankruptcy sale will have a reasonable chance of making a go of it.

Again, the exceptions to the rule abound, and if you have won the lottery then go right ahead and start your business from scratch. If you don't have a mortgage and don't have to worry about a guest coming through the front door, then have at it.

Then again, if you won the lottery, why do you want to clean toilets for a living? "Hey!" you say, *"I'm not going to clean toilets for a living! I'm the owner, and I'm going to hire good people to do that for me."* That is an excellent plan, and what could go wrong with that? Here is where a sarcasm font would be quite helpful.

Miscellaneous BEFORE

This is a miscellaneous catch all section. Think of it as a kitchen sink pizza: there will be something tasty in here somewhere for everyone, so grab a slice and settle in with a cold beer.

What's Inn a Name?

There are many things to consider when deciding what to name your property, but if you are smart you are buying a property with a good reputation and a solid business, and you would not change the name under any circumstances.

When Ruth Fertel bought the well-known Chris Steak House restaurant in the 1960's, she knew that she didn't want to lose the goodwill associated with the restaurant's name. So she only slightly modified it, calling the new business Ruth's Chris Steak House. It's a tongue twister and a story in itself, which has probably been told eight million times by her waiters, waitresses and bartenders.

Likewise, you may find yourself explaining the name of your property many, many times. How often do you think we told our tale? The "How did your inn get its name" conversation can be fun the first, say, dozen times. After 100 times, it will make you crazy. After 1,000 times, you'll need to get fitted for a straight jacket.

Q: How did the Salt Ash Inn get its name?
A: The town of Plymouth was originally incorporated as

the town of Saltash.

Q: Why did they change the town name from Saltash to
Plymouth?
A: There is a town near Plymouth, England with the
name Saltash.

Q How did *that* town get its name?
A: It might have come from the old English Salt Asa,
which describes the brackish area where fresh and salt
water meet.

Q: What does that have to do with it?
A: The town of Salt Ash in England is on a brackish river
like that.

Q: So it has nothing to do with salt mines over here?
A: No it does not.

Q: I thought it might have had something to do with the
burning of wood?
A: No, it doesn't

Q: Could there be any other meaning?
A: Yes, it could have come from "Essa," an early settler
family in Saltash, England.

Q: Anything else?
A: Or it could mean "Ash tree by the salt mill."

Q: You seem awfully confused.
A: Is that a question?

Q: No, not technically.
A: Okay.

I'm not telling you to avoid a property because it has a
goofy name, but if you are deciding between two
properties, I'd go with the generic name every time,
possibly with the name of the town in the title. If we had
been named "Ye Olde Friendly Plymouth Inn," I would
be a saner man today.

And while we're at it, avoid like the plague any name
with a pun. You'll note that I used a pun for this section,
"What's inn a name?" While I enjoy a good pun as much
as the next guy (a good pun is its own *reword*)
innkeeping advertising has flogged it like a dead horse. If
you have the willpower, please try to avoid using such
phrases as: inns and outs, innside joke, you'll fall inn
love, inncredible, and dewdrop inn. Consider it a public
service.

Staffing

Will you be hiring employees to help with the cleaning, cooking, yard work, shopping, laundry, bookkeeping, advertising, reservations, table waiting, bartending and check-ins? When you consider all of the jobs that you need to organize as innkeepers, it can begin to sound overwhelming. But don't worry, *it really is overwhelming.* Fortunately, you have the *entire 24 hours every day* to do these things.

Is the labor pool in the area large enough so that you can select your staff from the best candidates? When we first became innkeepers, we were so desperate for help that the only job requirement was a pulse. As we got pickier, we required our chamber staff to have their own transportation and a telephone. Once we finally broke the code and realized that we had to pay up for quality workers, our efficiency and professionalism skyrocketed to a top-notch level and we never looked back.

Competent, reliable and trained staff will be one of your keys to success. Your employees are the face of the business because you can't be in front of all of the guests all of the time. Make sure that you budget to keep the finest staff possible. Liza was with us for twelve years, Dennis for seven years, and many others for long periods of time.

If you are in a high volume tourist area (and if you are listening to us, you are) you will be competing with many other establishments for employees. Become known as a fair employer who pays a better than average wage and the best workers in the area will find you. Then when you write a book ten years after you sell your inn, your old employees won't come and punch you in the nose (they'll friend you on Facebook instead).

How Much Should I Pay for My Property?

Holy Toledo is that ever a big question! We're going to dance around this one like Fred and Ginger, and give you vague generalities because the answer will vary all over the map.

You will find that innkeepers think of their sales price as a per bedroom price. At the low end, a larger strip motel will be selling as cheaply as $10-$20k per bedroom. A midsized, average valued property will be in the $40-$70,000 per bedroom range, and the high end properties will easily be $125k *plus* per room. Consider these numbers very ballpark, and you will be evaluating the price tag with many other criteria, including inherent real estate value, current occupancy, profitability and expansion potential.

For the purposes of this book, we will use arbitrary (but not unreasonable) dollar amounts so that we can be on the same page when discussing cost benefit analyses. You have an *average sized* 12-bedroom property that you bought for $50k per bedroom and you are charging $100 a night (breakfast included) for two. For dinner, you earn $25 per person, and let's just say that includes beer and house wine. These prices can obviously be adjusted for your area.

Inn Brokers

Just as most transactions are financed and you'll need to work with a banker, most inns are purchased through a real estate broker who specializes in lodging properties. We bought our inn directly from the seller and sold directly to a buyer, but many times a broker will be involved; it can be done both ways.

When we were first looking to get into the innkeeping business, we stopped in a real estate office on the Killington Road and sat down with one of the agents. We told him that we were interested in becoming innkeepers, and could see him struggle not to roll his eyes at us. This was during the Bob Newhart innkeeping days, and I guess he saw quite a few of us wanna-bees sitting across from him every week.

He quickly, if politely, sent us on our way, telling us to "drive around and see what kind of properties we liked." Undaunted, we drove around with our clipboard and made notes. We came across the Salt Ash Inn and made a note that this was perfect! When we met with the broker the next day, we told him about the Salt Ash, and he said "Okay, but that one is not for sale, but now that I know what you are looking for we can focus our energy on that type of property."

We visited several properties with this broker, and learned more and more about ourselves and what we were looking for in a property. For that reason alone it is worth spending time with an inn broker. We could never quite find the right inn, however, so we decided to go back and knock on the door of the Salt Ash Inn. We asked the innkeepers if they had ever considered selling. They had. We bought.

PART II – AFTER YOU BUY

Now You're Stuck!

Holy crap! What have you done?

Wait, I'll come in again.

Congratulations!

You are now married to your business, for better or worse, for richer or poorer, in sickness and in health. It is time to focus on earning a profit so you can *stay* in business. Since these vows apparently offer a choice, let's work on avoiding the "worse, poorer and sick" options.

Airlines don't make money flying empty seats around the country, and you are not going to make money without heads on your pillows. Like the empty airline seat, an unused bedroom can never be resold. So you must focus on the most important part of innkeeping – the overnight guest – *THE BREAD IS IN THE BED!*

First, let's get on a little financial common ground so we can discuss numbers and how they relate to your decisions. Although I only made it halfway through the MBA program at Babson College, one of the most important things I took away from it was that *every decision has a price tag*. (Incidentally, I didn't finish graduate school because in the middle of the program we moved to Vermont to become innkeepers. I left the cozy womb of ivory tower academia, only to be cesarean-sectioned into the business world with a swift smack on the ass.)

One quick note about having a pub – guests do not stay with you *because* you have a bar, but they might *not* stay with you if you *don't* have one. It's not much of a profit center; so think of it as a service to your guests. If you want to make money in a bar, you'll need to buy a different book.

One caution regarding the pub area: don't let it get out of hand; bar business scares away room business. A nice relaxing place to grab a drink after the day is fine, but anything resembling the bar scene from the original *Star Wars* movie is too much.

In the expense department, the variable expenses associated with selling a room come from the cost of breakfast, linens, sheets, towels, wrapped paper cups (more on this later) and chamber maid service. This will cost you about $15 for the first night (half for supplies, half for room cleaning, and 25 cents for mints on the pillows) and $10 for every additional night after the first. And remember, you're charging your guest $100 per night.

The $25 dinner that you are selling is going to cost you about $15. You might think that's high, because a good restaurant is supposed to run at about a 33% food cost. Unless you are that restaurant (the subject of another business and another book) then you simply will not be as efficient. The focus of your business is not a restaurant, nor is it a pub, it is overnight lodging.

Traditionally, you change sheets halfway through a week-long stay, *or at the guests' request - no questions asked!* Repeat after me, the customer is always right (even when he is wrong.) When you see a sign at a country inn that says "additional towels will cost 50 cents," you know that the innkeeper has been frazzled down to his last nerve, and that you are probably stepping on it.

Speaking of signs, don't you love those "save the planet" signs that you see in motel bathrooms? If you could find it in your heart to not require your towels to be washed today, you will save the planet valuable water, save a baby seal from being clubbed, and save the whales from extinction. Nowhere on the card does it say that it saves the motel easy money by not replacing your towels. Go get some of these signs; Mother Nature thanks you.

How Do I Make Money TODAY?

While your guests are sleeping, go get a stout chain and secure their car's bumper to the nearest fence post.

If this is not possible (maybe you have run out of chains or fence posts) then try to figure out the next best thing that accomplishes the same goal. Go to the lost and found, get out the fuzzy handcuffs and shackle them to the bedpost. This may have the side benefit of helping you develop an entirely new client list. To my knowledge, bondage-trade niche market has yet to be tapped by the average country inn.

But I digress. The real goal here of course is that you want them to stay another night. How can you do this? Every situation will be different but here are a couple of ideas:

Opportunity Knocks

Offer a last-minute "extend your stay" opportunity. Tell your guests that you would love to have them for one more night, and ask if it is at all possible for them to rearrange their schedule. You'd like to offer them a 50% discount on their room tomorrow.

Be a salesperson! We can't tell you how many travelers out there are afflicted with "vacation brain" and would respond favorably to a good-natured invitation. Their schedules are often carved in marshmallow, and some genuine welcoming enthusiasm from an innkeeper may be all it takes to get them to stay with you for one more night.

Maybe you find it difficult to be a salesperson. It's not "quaint," whatever the hell that is. It somehow feels unseemly to ask a guest for his business. We urge you to get over that, and fast. You will be the most successful in your innkeeping life if you learn to ask *closing* questions. Don't ever lose sight of the fact that you are salespeople. You are just the kind that also makes omelets and fluffs pillows.

If you have to *ease* into this new salesperson mindset, for now you could put a sign in the front hall that says "This week only, extend your stay for 50% off the room rate," or "Tonight through Friday only, rooms $50 – and we'll throw in the breakfast!" This is just the innkeeper's version of "the take-away close." You've seen it on late-night TV: act now before supplies run out! I have a closet full of Ginsu knives that attest to the success of this close.

You don't want this lobby sign to look like the perpetual 50% off sale sign that you see at mattress stores. You don't want full price guests to feel that if they only had walked-in instead of making a reservation, you would have given them a better deal. So don't have this *temporary* sign on a brass plaque. Hand-write it and explain to the guests that this is a spur of the moment decision and a rare bird.

Here in Florida (where we now live), you would be embarrassed to go into Bed Bath and Beyond without the ubiquitous 20% off coupon. And nobody pays full price at Sea World where there are discounts in every newspaper and tourist pamphlet. Don't be foolish like these guys, you are not going to offer these special discounts to everybody all the time (it would lower the perceived value of your rooms).

But we will only let you get away with this passive salesmanship for a short time. The chapter on *How to Make Money this Year and Every Year* will include a few more closing ideas (as in sales closes) that you could adapt to your property. A complete treatise on closing situations is beyond the scope of this book, and shelves overflow with excellent books on how to be a better salesperson.

Although his advice is not specifically tailored toward the innkeeping industry, I recommend Tom Hopkins' _Sell it Today, Sell it Now_ (or pretty much anything he writes). Order it today (or with the magic of eBooks start reading it immediately). You can incorporate his advice into your customer service from this moment on.

Here's another idea to get them to stay: tell them that you are trying out a new menu item tomorrow, and if they could somehow rearrange their schedule to stay with you one more night, you would love to have them dine as your guests.

Do the math. If they stay in the room for one more night, dinner will cost you $30 and the room will cost you $10. Your variable expense room cost has been reduced because you are not changing the sheets; you are only cleaning the room (which usually gets finished quicker on stay-overs). So while you are "giving away" a free meal, you are actually earning $60. And they just might buy a bottle of nice wine to go with their "free" meal. We sold a lot of expensive wines on these nights.

The unquantifiable bonus is that you are helping them "make a memory" and giving them a nice story to share with their friends. If a guest has a good time at your inn, he may tell 3-5 friends. If he has a memorable time, he may tell 20-25 friends. If he has an awful time, he'll probably personally tell 100 people, put it on Yelp, and tweet it to the world until he gets it out of his system. Don't be the source of somebody's lousy vacation.

Here's another one: You can ask them if they have seen the play at the nearby playhouse? It was awesome, and you know this because you have gone to the opening night of all the shows (and you go to the shows because you are doing market research and trying to avoid burnout at the same time). Tell them that there are still tickets available (because you called this morning) and you'd love to make the arrangements for them.

Or this one: You can tell them that you have a bet with three other innkeepers that you can get more people to extend their stay than they can. You're a very competitive person and you'll do whatever it takes to beat them. (And go ahead and make this bet. It's fun!) Tell them you'll do anything. Ask them what they would do, if they were in your shoes, to talk the next guest into staying another evening. Get them involved and excited about trying to help you with your occupancy bet. If they were on the fence as to where to go next, they might just *do you a favor* and stay with you. And maybe you'll get some new ideas as well; you'd be surprised at the number of creative people who walk through your front door.

I'll Write You a Note

I must have used this one a thousand times over the years to try to get a guest to stay with us one more night. Our inn was popular on the weekends and everybody knows the fun of a three-day weekend. Sometimes all it took to nudge a guest into staying over on Sunday night and not going to work the next day was a little assistance from his friendly innkeeper.

For whatever reason, snow forecast, sun forecast, or a distinct possibility that the rapture will not be happening forecast, I would say to a guest at Sunday morning breakfast, "How would you like to spend another night with us?" (Or you could start with humor, taking a line from our friend Faith, and say *"Don't let Monday morning ruin your Sunday night!"*)

Odds are, when you ask them if they want to stay, they will say something like *"We'd love to, but we can't"* and offer up their reason (most likely a good one). Then I would say, "Well okay, maybe next time" and walk away and never ask them again.

If you think that is not actually what I did, then you *have* been paying attention.

I would reinforce my original invitation with a "But it's *really* going to be *'whatever'* tomorrow!" And then, as if inspiration is striking me for the very first time, I would say, "Tell you what, I'll write your boss (or wife or husband) a note!"

Then we would all laugh. Then I would shut up and look at them. What happened? In the sales world, I had just asked a closing question. It is critical that once you ask a closing question, you keep your mouth shut. You *never* talk yourself out of a possible sale.

Innkeepers like to talk, and I think they probably talk themselves out of too many sales. So here's the *biggest piece of innkeeper sales advice* in this book: once you've asked a closing question - SHUT UP!

There might be a pause in the conversation, but it is not necessarily awkward. You've just made a joke, and you are all sitting back and enjoying the moment. But what is really happening in the back of the guests' minds is that they are *thinking it over*. We had hundreds of guests stay over with us with "spur of the moment" decisions, so be ready to encourage them.

Of course it wasn't really spur of the moment. If you had been doing your job, they were in their rooms talking about what a nice time they were having and wishing that they could continue. They might have already discussed the possibility of staying another night, but it hadn't really been a concrete plan, just a nice idea. Maybe they'd try you again sometime (and yes, they probably would).

What you did was introduce the reality of, hey, this could be real! Why the heck not spend another night? The innkeeper likes us and we like it here and hey, I've got a vacation day coming, or I feel the sniffles coming on.

Just to mix it up every once in a while I would tell the guest "Hey, you're looking a little under the weather. I'm pretty sure that you need to stay another day just to rest up!" (Laugh) "I'll write you a note!" (More laughter.) I'm sure your boss would be fine with a note from your innkeeper.

Did I stop there? Well, let's not beat a dead horse; you know that I didn't. Before they had a chance to get buyer's remorse I would reinforce their decision. With a huge smile (and some entertaining over-acting) I would say, *"Welcome Back!"* We would all laugh because now *I* am the one looking silly instead of *them* feeling silly for being able to be talked into staying another day. (The truth is, they *will* enjoy another day at your inn because you are doing your job.)

I'd tell them that I'd check the reservation book and see if they can keep their room for the rest of the month. (More laughing.) Usually I would get a smiling, "No, tonight will be enough." That's really all I wanted, to reinforce that they are indeed spending another night with us. And it's not that big a deal, right? It's not another month, it's just another night. We were having a too much fun, anyway.

And in the distance, you can hear your bank account relax with a satisfied, *"That'll do pig. That'll do."* (If you didn't see the movie _Babe_, then this last reference probably convinced you that I'm nuts. Go rent the movie and come back and re-read the sentence. It's perfect. Trust me.)

How Do I Make Money THIS MONTH?

There are certain strategies that you can use *immediately* to help bring money in the door sooner rather than later. The next section - *How to Make Money This Year and Every Year* - will focus on more long-term strategies that you will be using to *stay* profitable.

My Itinerary Runneth Over

Don't *just* offer a list of suggestions for things to see and do in the area. Take it to the next level and have a thick binder of *"Incredible Day Trips"* from your property. Show your guests that they have barely scratched the surface of the things to see and do your area, and that you could keep them busy *for weeks* if they had the time to stay.

What we settled on, and this will work for anybody, is putting together itineraries that jam pack the fun into day long (*and tiring*) trips. Find every attraction within 2 to 3 hours' drive time and group them together into a see-and-do list.

Maybe there are antique stores in dozens of nearby towns. Maybe there are brew pubs (designated driver required!) Maybe there are historic sites, chairlift rides, hiking trails, covered bridges, beaches, wineries, breweries, spas, and many fine restaurants. The point is, you know what is in your area and you know that you want to fill people's days with fun so they come back tired looking for their pillows.

Every Vermont innkeeper knows to send people to the Ben and Jerry's factory for ice cream. But even this is still only just a day trip like the Calvin Coolidge Homestead. As much as you love ice cream, you're not going to visit the factory two days in a row. But when you start putting these day trips together into packages, you can fill up your guests' days nicely.

You're going to start working on your packages and putting these itineraries in your front hallway, in your room books, and on your webpage.

For example, I had one package that sent the guests to the Calvin Coolidge Homestead for the morning, up to the middle of Vermont for lunch with Ben and Jerry, over to another quaint town to explore a glassblowing factory, and then back to the inn. The next day I had another package that sent them in a different direction to another town, an antique store, a playhouse, a cider mill, and a summer chair lift ride.

I bet that you could list dozens of interesting activities within a couple of hours of your property. It's one thing to just tell the vacationing public that there are many things to see and do in your area. Take it to that critical next level: hand them an itinerary with mileage, drive times, admission costs, shows and show times, and recommended restaurants. You get the idea.

We used to call it "vacation brain," and we get it ourselves when we go away. That's when you put all of your thinking on hold for a while and relax. We laughed when the first guest early in our career asked us after breakfast, "What should we do today?" (*It's your vacation; do whatever you want!*) After hearing this question enough times, it dawned on us that we had better have a much more complete answer than something that occurred to us just off the top of our heads.

Guests can either do the same thing over and over (like ski or bicycle) or you can give them multiple itineraries to keep them returning to the house each evening. Repeat after me, *THE BREAD IS IN THE BED.* You need to give them enough things to do during the day so that they stay in their bed another night or three.

You're not being a sneaky innkeeper here. It's just good common sense, and the guests will love you for it! Remember, they are afflicted with vacation brain and they need Dr. Itinerary to help them. The life you save may be your own.

Friends and Family

Maybe you are not the consummate salesman (yet). So why don't you start with the people you know - your friends and family? There is a reason that insurance agencies hire new agents by the bucket load. The new agents will sell policies to all of their friends and families, and then if they are any good, will start to sell policies to the public. If the new agent fails to succeed in the business, at least the agency has a few dozen more policies. This same system works well for another organization that sells a lot of *thin mint cookies* every year.

We are not saying to have your BFFs pay to stay with you, but you can use their goodwill to help you get business. It is likely that most of your close friends and family know that you are now keeping an inn. If not, shout it from the mountain tops and invite them to come see you! It will be like tossing a huge boulder into a pond and spreading advertising ripples everywhere. You'll find that your friends think it's pretty neat (if not half-crazy) that you have decided to chuck it all and become an innkeeper. It's a fun story for them to tell their *other* friends, who will in turn pass along your saga to the many people who *they* know.

We had a standing rule with friends and relatives that they could stay for free if the inn was not filled. If we were going to be filled, then they had the choice to either pay for the room or sleep on a mattress on the Owner's Quarters living room floor.

We had hundreds of paying guests over the years who were told to come see us because we were friends of friends. It is fun, gratifying *and profitable* to set fire to this word-of-mouth source of advertising.

We hosted a "Cousin's Reunion" at the inn, inviting our relatives to come stay with us during a slow period. It was great fun and served two purposes, one unintended. Our cousin's reunion brought the mountain to Mohammed because as innkeepers we kept missing family reunions. The only way that we could see our relatives seemed to be to gather them under *our* roof on *our* timeline. It allowed our relatives to personally see the inn, and they could tell *their* friends about it firsthand. As I recall, we charged a couple of bucks to help pay the cost of food, pub, sheets and towels, but it was family fun that paid unexpected dividends over the years.

Another group came from my brother Ron. He is in the 33rd year of a fantasy football league, which started long before they even called it fantasy football. About a dozen of his college buddies get together each year for a cigar- and beer-filled live draft. Ron suggested that they hold one of their drafts in Vermont, and we had an instant twelve room reservation block. Sure, we gave free beer, but at twenty cents a glass it didn't hurt too badly. Ron was a perpetual ambassador for us, and we had overnight guests from as far back as his high school days.

Get your peeps up to the inn as soon as possible. Invite your friends and relatives; get them on your side and send them out into the world as your marketing representatives. They will all be goodwill ambassadors for you wherever they go. It's one thing to say that your friend or cousin owns an inn, but quite another to say that you spent a wonderful weekend there and here are some great things that you can do when *you* visit.

Don't underestimate the friend factor when it comes to staffing. I preyed upon fraternity brothers over the years for assistance (John designed the cover for this book). In our first year my "little brother" Brian ran the restaurant, bringing order from chaos. He had managerial training in a chain establishment (that served square hamburgers) and was able to bring those skills to the inn. Dr. Petey (and *his* brother Danny Boy) filled in as bartenders quite a few times. Alan was a regular, and somehow was around for several big events, including the deer rampage. Dennis helped on many weekends before he finally just decided to not check-out. He stayed with us for seven years and we couldn't have done it without him (don't tell him, he'll get a big head).

Woof - Going to the Dogs

If you are not "pet friendly" yet, you might consider allowing pets into a room or two located conveniently near an exit. The pet traveling public is having an increasingly difficult time finding *country inns* that will accept pets. We found that they don't expect the pets to be allowed into the common areas; just in the rooms will be fine. You can develop quite a reputation in the pet traveling world as these owners have an extensive social network who are trying to find interesting properties and still bring Fido.

Once you decide that you are going to the dogs (or cats, or iguanas), tell every inn and motel within fifteen miles of your front door. Bring them a little stack of pre-printed cards with the words "pet friendly" and a map to your location. You will cultivate a great pet friendly reputation locally, and your fellow innkeepers will thank you for it. They will benefit because they get to do a service for someone who (this time) can't stay with them. Then it's up to you to show this guest why *your* inn is nicer than your friend's inn. What can we say, it's a dog eat dog world out there.

Bounty – Sounds so Much Nicer Than "Bribe"

Unless the "No" sign is Gorilla glued to the word "Vacancy," you should consider this strategy.

We made a bunch of business size cards with our information on them and the note "10% off tonight only" and gave them to the front registration counters at the larger hotels in the area. We gave them personally to the employees that worked the check-in desks. We told them that if for whatever reason they have a guest that they cannot accommodate, we would love to help them. Here's a card with directions to our property and we will give them 10% off (limited to selected dates). And please put your name on the bottom of the card, because we would like to give you a $20 thank you for sending them to us. Is this unseemly? Who knows? But it worked. And we made some friends at the check-in desks at the big motels in the area, which sure didn't hurt.

The Reservation Card Gold Mine

Do your old check-in slips sit in a shoebox (physical or virtual) and gather dust until you get to your mailing list someday? Are you diligent about keeping in contact with your alumni? If you see a hole in the schedule, you may want to send a targeted mailing (email or postal) to everyone who was a guest of your inn during this exact month in the previous two years.

If you are a new innkeeper, spend time making sure that the mailing list is current, and introduce yourself to the previous guests with a letter. They would love to hear about you and you can tell them how you look forward to having them visit the inn to meet you.

We admit that at first we were not as diligent with our mailing list as we should have been. Once we brought it up to date, we would bulk mail newsletters to our guests and the phones would start ringing again. You could (also) send an email blast, but remember that people might be more likely to read your newsletter if it comes in their postal mailbox.

How Do I Make Money THIS YEAR And Every Year After?

Our favorite cookbooks in the world are put out by *Cook's Illustrated*. They are more than just cookbooks because they tell you not only what works in the recipe, but what they tried to do that *didn't work*. That is what we will do in this chapter. We'll tell you our success stories and our failures (comical and sometimes naïvely embarrassing). After a while, you'll get a flavor of what worked and what didn't. The important thing is to <u>keep trying</u>.

I gave a high school graduation speech that included the poem *Don't Quit* (author unknown). I won't bore you with the whole thing (as I bored the auditorium that evening), but here is the first stanza that you might want to put on your mirror (or have tattooed on your wrist):

DON'T QUIT

When things go wrong, as they sometimes will,
When the road you're trudging seems all uphill,
When the funds are low and the debts are high,
And you want to smile, but you have to sigh,
When care is pressing you down a bit,
Rest, if you must, but don't you quit.

These were back in the days when graduation speeches could be corny. Even back in my high school years I could sense that persistence was going to pay off in life.

When we bought our inn, it had been closed during the summer months while the previous innkeepers worked on other businesses that they had going. The innkeepers would reopen for the fall foliage season which was excellent business all over Vermont. In fact, on Columbus Day weekend the nearest open room "in Vermont" was probably somewhere down in Connecticut.

Throughout our first summer, we did not know what to expect in terms of guest volume. The previous innkeepers were not focusing on inn revenues from April through August. We consulted our business plan, which told us that the Calvin Coolidge Homestead was going to be a gold mine, and you know how that turned out.

But we kept plugging away trying everything that we could think of to increase the summer revenues. Some things worked, some things didn't, which is the freshman curriculum at Hard Knocks University.

Get the Groups

Some Ideas Do Work – Vermont Bicycle Tours

Here's a great story that illustrates how being persistent, never being quite satisfied, and always delivering the best possible product helped our business tremendously.

One of the first things that we noticed when we bought the inn (it was hard not to notice!) were all of the bicyclists that passed by every day. It didn't take long before we discovered that these were organized bike tours, and that they traveled from inn to inn over the course of a week.

You don't need to be Thomas Edison to see the light bulb that went off over my head. I immediately contacted one bicycle touring company whose vans we were always seeing (Vermont Bicycle Tours) and told them that our inn, previously closed in the summer times, was now open for business and we would love for them to give us a try!

They thanked me politely for my call, but told me that their brochures are produced a year in advance and their tours were already pretty well set. I said, "Oh well, thank you anyway," and never spoke with them again.

Not!

Since they could not use us for overnights, we asked VBT if they would consider using us as a lunch stop. The typical bike tour does not have a formal lunch stop as bicyclists plod along at their own paces throughout the day; however they were happy to put us in the tour notes for the groups that passed us. These notes were much more up to the minute and were given to the leaders so they could tell their guests what to expect each day. It was easy for them to say that there's a quaint little inn along the route that will serve you lunch in a pub. It wasn't a head in a bed, but it was definitely a foot in a door.

It turns out that just as McDonald's has its Burger King, VBT has its VCC (Vermont Country Cyclers.) Vermont Bicycle Tours was the first and the largest, but VCC had a pretty good business going as well. The bike tour business was so popular that there were another half a dozen fledgling bike tour companies that tried to piggyback off of the success of the big guns.

So while we were able to serve hundreds of lunches that first year, what we really wanted was for VBT to try us for an overnight tour. We drove around, consulted with the bicyclists about which roads they liked and why, and put together a two-night list of routes that would be possible for VBT to use.

We presented them with a two-night tour package possibility, complete with routes, mileage, things to see and do along the way, and photos of what their guests would see at the inn and in the area. We also priced the package very competitively to entice them to at least give us a try.

Well, VBT tried us for *one* tour weekend the next year – it was called the Plymouth Roundabout. It was offered on every weekend in the foliage season (which we could have booked anyway) and a few times earlier in the summer (when we would not be booked). We decided that it would be worth the trade-off, giving VBT our foliage weekends even though we would make more money selling rooms to the run-of-the-mill non-cycling public.

We needed to get our foot in the VBT door and were willing to make the foliage revenue sacrifice to do it. On the Plymouth Roundabout guests would arrive for Friday night dinner, bicycle on Saturday, have dinner on Saturday night, then bicycle Sunday and leave late in the afternoon after bicycling. They would check out of their rooms on Sunday morning, and we would have two bedrooms available for afternoon showering.

(As you might guess, we did everything we could to sell the VBT guests a Sunday night room. We told them that we could keep "their room" available when they came back at the end of the day's cycling. That way they wouldn't have to rush their Sunday cycling or have to shower in the common shower rooms.)

In the spirit of more is better, we suggested to VBT that they try to offer this tour during the mid-weeks. At first they were reluctant, as they need a minimum of four guests to break even on the tours, and they were not sure if mid-week 2-day business was viable.

The only mid-week tours that they ever offered were 5-days long. Everyone "knew" that mid-weeks were for 5-day tours, and any suggestion of a mid-week 2-day tour was sheer heresy! Well, we can be pretty persistent, and eventually got them to try a few Wednesday/Thursday night Plymouth Roundabouts.

Low and behold, there was indeed a market for a mid-week 2-day tour, and the Plymouth Roundabout mid-week became as popular as the weekend tour; that is, it was usually full!

Let's pause here for some hungry hiker humor. I promise it will tie in to the story. On the Appalachian Trail there are three kinds of hikers: the *day hiker* or average Joe who will go out for a day or two; the *section-hiker* who will go out for a week or two; and the *thru-hiker*, who is intending to hike all 2,180 miles in a year. What's the difference between these hikers? A day hiker is strolling down the trail and sees an M&M in front of him, steps over it and keeps walking. The section-hiker comes along, picks it up, eats it and goes on his way. A thru-hiker coming up to the same M&M, will pick it up, eat it and start digging around in the dirt looking for more.

So do you think that we were satisfied with four nights a week booked with bicycle tours? Absolutely not! There were still three more days of the week unclaimed. We got out the VBT and the VCC catalogs and charted the tour's that were in our area for the 5-day tours. We used our imagination to find how we could stretch their tour routes so they could stay with us.

Then we called the companies and told them our great plan. By this time we were great friends with the VBT tour leaders, and they were quite helpful in our market research. They knew what 5-day tours might be altered and what inns might not be providing the level of customer service that we were providing. (I will also say that in fourteen years of hosting bike tours, a leader never paid for a beer. So you might use your imagination as to one of the reasons they liked us so much.)

Within two years we had all seven nights of the week booked with bicycle tours (six with VBT, one with VCC). Every tour did not run every week, but each night of the week was scheduled with a tour.

Do you think we were finally satisfied? Of course not! Now you're getting the idea. Keep digging; there might be another M&M in there somewhere. We looked at the Wed/Thur schedule and tried to get VBT to schedule more five-day tours on weeks that the mid-week Plymouth Roundabout was not slated to run.

This did not happen during the first year of course. It took years of developing a relationship with them, but after a while they knew that they could count on us to keep their guests happy. The operating manager of VBT paid us one of the greatest compliments we ever received. *He said that he never gave our tours a second thought.* They were worry free for him, and he knew that his customers (and there were many hundreds of them over the years) would be extremely pleased with their stay. With a relationship like that you can see why VBT was willing to schedule their five-day tours around our availability, illustrating how the combination of persistence and commitment to excellence pays off for your business.

Once we had their guests at the inn, we did absolutely everything we could to make them happy. By the time we left the inn fourteen years after the first tour, *we were VBT's most used inn and had been for about nine years in a row.* We tried to do the same with other tour companies, and had varying degrees of success with them as well. But VBT was the big dog, and the big dog ate with us.

Because of our bike tour success, the summer/fall season turned out to be as strong as our winter, with 70 -90 plus bike tour *overnights* each year. That is saying something as the lodging in our area was primarily built around the winter tourism.

We were in ski country, where winter travelers strapped sticks to the top of their cars and came to beat themselves up on the Vermont hillsides. They did this every weekend, and many of them could do it for five days at a time. (*"As we dance to the masochism tango,"* sings Tom Lehrer.)

One (unusual) day we woke up to a blistering cold outside temperature of *30 degrees below zero*! Undaunted, several of our fanatical skiing guests stacked their car batteries around the pub's circular fireplace to heat them so they could start their cars and get to the slopes. The smarter ones took the hint from Mother Nature and stayed in the pub all day.

You might not have a ski resort in your backyard, and maybe your inn is not perfect for bicycling (or maybe it is) but there certainly are things to do in your neck of the woods. You've been telling your guests about them for years. What do skiers and bicyclists have in common? Other than being stinky at the end of the day? They come back to your inn each night pooped out! Except for the occasional broken bone, it's generally what people refer to as a "good tired."

So we racked our brains to try to figure out how *else* we might poop out the guests, and came up with a not so brilliant idea: Vermont Golf Tours.

Some Ideas Don't Work - Vermont Golf Tours (VGT)
Not everything we did turned to gold (far from it). Even
the best baseball players only get on base one-third of the
time, and we swung and missed with quite a few
marketing efforts over the years. One of the more fun
"misses" was with a golf club. Whiff!

Since there were excellent golf courses located ten miles
in every direction from the inn, we tried to put together
golf tour packages modeled after VBT's business plan.
While these packages did produce a modicum of success,
the whole idea never really succeeded. But we had a lot
of fun "market researching" the golf courses and
designing the golf shirts.

We met with an artist and told him we wanted to
combine something ubiquitous in Vermont with the game
of golf. We settled on a golfing cow. When the first
drawings came back we had tears in our eyes from
laughing so hard. They showed a golfing cow in full
swing, with udders flying in the breeze.

Thinking that the udders might be misinterpreted when
embroidered on a golf shirt, we put knickers on the cow.
That was even funnier. The golf shirts were wonderful
and were big sellers, but they never did put many golfers'
heads in our beds. In 20/20 hindsight, we should have put
the name of the inn underneath the VGT logo. People
were snapping up the shirts just for the cow, which was
udderly ridiculous.

Group Spinoffs – Double Your Fun

TV shows are famous for their spinoffs, and you should be too. *All In the Family* spun off *The Jeffersons*; *Cheers* spun off *Frasier*; *Gray's Anatomy* spun off *Private Practice*, and *Keeping up with the Kardashians* spun off *Kourtney and Khloe' Take Miami*.

When groups arrive, there may be a few people who have never even heard of you, and are only at your inn because their group is staying with you. As you are the consummate innkeeper and marketer continually looking for another source of new business, your marketing antennae should go up. There is bound to be someone who is pleasantly surprised with "their discovery" of your inn. Since they are already in a group, they are seeing how well your property works for groups and some are thinking to themselves "Hey I could bring my friends/coworkers/customers here, too!" We had many new groups over the years that were led by people who came as guests in previous groups.

Try to double your pleasure with the groups that you have. They already like you - that's why they're there in the first place! Maybe the group would like to come back *twice* in one year; it never hurts to ask!

We were so popular with a certain financial magazine (let's call it *"Real Intelligent" Money*) that they booked two weekends each year. But it didn't start that way; in fact we didn't even find the group in the first place; they were a *spinoff* from a VBT tour!

While chatting with the magazine staff at the bar during the bike tour, I suggested that they bring their customers back for a ski trip. They like to thank their customers all year round, don't they? By the time the bike tour ended, we had another group booked for the winter. The second year the magazine booked two winter tours – one for advertisers and one for a staff "thank you" party.

They continued to visit us twice a year for many seasons (sometimes once in the summer and once in the winter, other times for two winter groups). Once *they* spun off an online magazine from their printed magazine, we got *that* new group to stay with us as well. Is all this spinning making you dizzy, too?

Another of our favorite *spinoff* groups was an industrial company that designed and produced saw blades. Every year they would come up for a working business week, and unlike some boondoggle trips, these people really worked eight-plus hours a day. They took over the whole property, so we arranged the common areas into work areas. We hung out a "Closed for Private Party" sign for the whole week and gave this group the complete run of the inn.

We cooked breakfast, lunch and dinner for them and basically did everything we could to make their working vacation successful. Our trip was so well received at their company that another division started booking week-long work groups with us. So when you are hosting a group, keep asking yourself if there is other business that you can develop with the people who are already under your roof.

We had a church group that booked twice each year, early and late ski season. These came about because we sat down with the group leaders and asked if it was possible that they would consider visiting us again. So nice, they did it twice! Don't just focus on surviving through the groups, although that will be tempting. You are the Appalachian Trail thru-hiker of marketing, digging for more M&Ms.

Be Memorable

We read a lot of advice telling you to make sure your inn reflects the area in which you are located. If you are at the beach, you should have nice ocean pictures in your room and maybe a model of a ship in the hallway. To us, that kind of thinking just helps you blend in with everybody else. You don't want to camouflage your inn so much that it doesn't stand out from the neighbors!

We learned this lesson only by a stroke of luck early in our innkeeping career (a "blind squirrel getting the acorn" moment.) When we bought the inn, it was a nice big white building with black shutters and a red barn. There was a row of seven white Adirondack chairs on the front porch which looked very inviting behind Ann's gorgeous flower beds.

Business was slow, so Ann decided to go down to Boston to visit her parents. While she was away, I thought that I would surprise her. (*"Hey, I've got a great idea!"*) Going on the theory that it is easier to ask for forgiveness than to get permission, I went to the local hardware store and purchased seven quarts of paint in the colors of the rainbow, painted each Adirondack chair a different color, and arranged them in the order Mr. Biv would have wanted (you remember Roy G. Biv, right - the guy who invented the rainbow?)

When Ann got back to Vermont, she was not entirely thrilled with my juvenile "decorating" idea. Soon, however, we started to notice people stopping their cars, getting out and taking photographs - this had not been the standard practice of the photographic traveler up until then. We figured that people were tired of driving around New England seeing white houses and with black shutters and red barns. They wanted to use some of the color in their film (back in the days of film).

Before long, the biggest newspaper in the state had our photo on the front page of a Sunday issue, we were picked up in many travel magazines, coffee table books and even a few calendars. Once a Peter Pan tour bus ejected 40-plus tourists to photograph the chairs (hey, they stopped the bus first!) I was so flabbergasted that I forgot to get *my* camera out to take a picture of *them*.

If you see multi-colored Adirondack chairs today, it was a trend that started at our inn in 1986. Too bad you can't patent whimsy.

To this day, this is the only time that Ann has ever needed to utter the words "*you were right, honey, and I was wrong.*" Even though it was 27 years ago, I cherish the moment as if it was yesterday. (Still love you, honey.)

The next year, we painted our large front yard sign in matching red, orange, yellow, green and blue. If a little is good, a lot is better, right? So think of something memorable - paint your inn emergency orange! Or not. The point is, think of something to make you stand out from the crowd. Then put it on a t-shirt!

We had one guest joke that she already had *two* babies thanks to us. We didn't want to take *all* the credit, but we did come up with a tongue-in-cheek "fertility package" that included a candle, bottle of champagne, CD player with *Kenny G*, and some things we probably shouldn't mention in a family publication. We didn't have this package because we wanted to become a breeding clinic. We just thought it would be fun and *memorable* and would give people an amusing story to tell others about the inn.

The point is, if you want your property to be memorable, stand out from the crowd. If you're not going to be a black sheep, be a rainbow sheep! Think back on memorable properties that you have seen.

We have been to hundreds of inns over the years, and even though we visited them for only one night over thirty years ago, this is one property that still stands out: the Madonna Inn in San Luis Obispo, California has taken "memorable" to steroid-laden extremes. They have dozens of individually decorated suites that look as if they were created by a Hollywood movie set designer. There are monstrous fireplaces in several rooms; one room has stone walls and ceilings; there is an over-the-top gaudy yet fun restaurant, and a waterfall urinal in the men's room. Getting to urinate (legally) into a waterfall is something I'll never forget.

Many little things can be memorable, too. Ann's wildflower garden produced an endless supply of edible flowers for the dinner plates. Our guests were fascinated, and they regularly asked us if the flowers were edible. Our running joke was that we hoped that *everything* we served was edible!

We had our own ghost story of an old stagecoach traveler who would appear in your guest room. You'd know it was him because he only appeared from the waist up.

We had one room with a door to what once led to a fancy "second floor outhouse." It now leads to an outside wall, but previous innkeepers were smart enough to keep the door intact for the "memorable" department.

Open House for Locals

You can bet that the neighbors are curious as to what your property looks like inside. Sometimes they might feel strange asking to come in for a tour when they just live in the neighborhood. Have a public open house and invite everybody over for a party. Feed them appetizers and have some music going to make it an event.

Then when they have out-of-town friends, relatives or guests, who do you think they're going to call? You want your inn to be the first one that comes to mind. And go ahead and tell them why you're having this party. We want to steal your friends! Give your family to us!

You could even offer deeply discounted rooms for locals who just want to try you for an overnight. That way they are sure to have their family or friends stay with you because they know what a great place you have. You may make a few dollars on the room, but the point is that this is a marketing expense. Give them your $100 room for $50 and ask them to please remember you when their relatives come to town.

Embrace New Technology

If you have Twitter or Facebook followers, what better way to instantly tell them that "all of a sudden" you have an open room for the weekend? We asked guests if they wanted to be on our "last minute cancellation list" so we could alert them when we had a room open. Even if they couldn't travel on the spur of the moment, these email blasts reinforced our name in their minds.

Nothing ever dies on the internet; it's the closest we'll get to living forever! Check out our old webpages from the 1990's by Googling "wayback machine" and search for vermontvacation.com. Among other things, there is a January 1998 page with a Top 10 LIST giving advice to prospective innkeepers. I still agree with nine of them, which proves that good advice is timeless. (I've included these TOP 10 LISTS from the 1990's in **Addendum 2**.)

These webpages were written before there was such a company as Google. Now Google is taking over the planet and we are even "verbing" them: I Googled; you Googled; she Googled; we had fun Googling our pluperfect lives away.

Back in the dinosaur days, I remember one innkeeper association meeting where we gave a brief little spiel to the other innkeepers about this new thing coming along called the "internet," and how easy it was to have an online brochure. Half of the innkeepers thought it would be a waste of time, and the other half thought it would be pretty neat, so we volunteered to do webpages for anybody who wanted one. A few innkeepers took us up on it and we put up what amounted to an online copy of their written brochures. That was the most anybody - at that time - wanted to do with the internet.

I took our page further, realizing that it was like a bottomless brochure, and if I could not "*dazzle them with brilliance, I could baffle them with baloney.*" More is better; go Y- chromosomes! And as is my nature, I started filling up my webpage with things to do in the area, Top 10 lists of innkeeping life (Letterman was popular back then, too) and dozens of photographs. Then, as now, it was very expensive to print and mail someone a four-color brochure. Directing them to the webpage was easy.

It will come as no surprise when we say that you absolutely *must* have a webpage. Almost everyone has one now, and it really is no big deal anymore. But you need to stay ahead of the curve. You need to have an online presence in *all* of the new technologies as they come down the road. You need to be on Facebook, Twitter, Pinterest and whatever else might become the latest and greatest.

We understand that you are too busy putting blueberries on pancakes to keep up with all of this computer stuff. That is why you are going to rent a teenager from the local high school (or one from one of your friends, neighbors or relatives.) Maybe you are "lucky" enough to have a teenager in the house. Kids today have been lapping this stuff up with mother's milk and it is second nature to them.

For the total investment of Mountain Dew, Doritos and a few bucks you can be brought up to speed, and the little monsters can show you how to update your online pages with just the click of a button. Just don't "Friend" your kids; they will die of embarrassment and you'll have funeral expenses to fit into the budget.

Put a computer workstation in your common area and offer free hors d'oeuvres to people who will "Like" you on Facebook. Tell them it's a bribe! I'm sure that many of your guests would love to help.

There is one time when "going viral" can be a good thing. It's when people spread the word so quickly about you that there are groups of people who learn about you that you never planned to reach. Your webpage can have a "Share Button" that will allow visitors to tell their friends about you. With any luck, they'll tell *their* friends, who will tell *their* friends, etc. Your Share button can have links to: Facebook, StumbleUpon, MySpace, Blogger, Pinterest, Linkedin, Twitter, Tumblr and *hundreds* more.

As my niece Becky (yet another techie kid) said to me back when she was 7-years old and we were in line at the Tower of Terror at Disney World, "I have to face my fears, Uncle Glen." I urge you to face your fears and keep up with the tech stuff.

Expand Your Hobby – Beer, Anyone?

Do you have a hobby that might bring guests to your inn? With the microbrewery craze in Vermont, it was easy to get excited about craft-brewed beers. We had ten beers on tap in the pub, the majority of them brewed somewhere in Vermont. There was a niche traveler that was coming to the area and visiting the breweries and the brewpubs. As we were home brewers, we thought it might be fun to offer our beer at the bar. In order to do that, we needed to get a federal license.

Getting a brewpub license for a tiny bar in Vermont was pretty interesting. It was not expensive, but there was a mountain of government paperwork that we had to go through in order to be approved. We had to fill out the same paperwork that Budweiser had to fill out if they wanted to open a new plant somewhere.

It was quite comical filling out some of the questions. One asked how much energy we would be using in a calendar year, "For example, 200,000 tons of bituminous coal." I put my pitiful answer in the blank next to it: *10 gallons of propane.*

When the Bureau of Alcohol, Tobacco and Firearms sent an agent to interview us, the guy asked if this was a joke. We assured him that we were indeed serious, and he then completed the paperwork with a tiny grin. The BATF wanted to make sure that there was no illegal money being used to finance a new alcohol-related business (or as Hawkeye Pierce once said, "Ill-gotten booty; or ill-booten gotty").

We explained that we already owned the equipment and we were brewing in our kitchen. There would be no financing involved. Apparently there is not a check box for such a bizarre situation on the government paperwork.

Eventually we got our license, and our advertising soon touted us as the smallest brewpub in Vermont (and possibly the world). Budweiser spilled in an hour what we brewed in a year. It was never our intention to become a public bar, and that is why our advertising highlighted our central location to the *other* breweries and brewpubs in Vermont. As long as the beer drinking traveler was coming to Vermont to visit these establishments, where was he going to lay his head? At a brewpub and inn of course!

Maybe there is a hobby of yours that you can "tap" into to find another source of guests. It does not have to be beer, it could be doll collectors, ice cream eaters, sewing circles or the People With Too Much Money Society. Use your imagination and keep trying to find a niche. While golf tours might have failed, the brewpub did quite well putting more heads in our beds.

Weddings – I Do or I Don't?

Innkeepers either love or hate weddings. We were in the latter category, since weddings usually filled us up with people who would not necessarily choose to spend time with us in the first place. The bride may have loved us, but we were not automatically her guest's cup of tea. They didn't pick us out of dozens of inns; they were staying with us because the bride told them to.

It doesn't mean that you don't have the opportunity to try to attract more long-term business, but as a rule the wedding guests are focused on many other things (as they should be) and the inn is the least of their concerns. But, they *are* blocks of rooms and do meet the criteria of bringing in groups, so they are viable.

We would advise you to *never host a wedding or reception* unless that is the focus of your business. Like a black hole, it will gobble a lot of your time and energy while you are trying to take care of other guests in other weeks, even if the Bride is not a Zilla.

Frequent Fliers

You're not a prison (I hope), so you want a high recidivism rate. Outside of bike tours, an incredible 80% of our guests were either other groups, repeat customers or were specifically told to come see us by a previous guest. This is an extraordinary number, and you need to strive to get this same high percentage of repeat and referral business.

Reward your best guests so they keep coming back, and there are many ways that you can do this. You can have a policy that every 5th night is free. You can (at the spur of the moment) tell them that their next night will be free if they can stay. I encourage you to use this one a lot. If you have a room available and you know it's only going to cost you ten dollars to keep a good customer in the house and strengthen your relationship with them, by all means go for it!

You could offer them a room category upgrade after their third stay of the year. This worked for us because we had four categories of rooms: economy, standard, deluxe, and a deluxe suite. You could give them the "double upgrade" which makes them feel great and does not cost you a single penny more.

We are generally fans of staying at country inns, but there is one big chain that we like: Loews. They have blue, gold, silver and platinum levels depending on your number of stays with them. They have a couple of resorts near Universal Studios (one of our favorite places) and we stay at one of their hotels whenever we pass through Orlando. We were proud of ourselves for reaching their gold level, but one night we had a challenge in our room. The specifics aren't important, other than to say that the management was professional when we explained our difficulties the next morning. As a courtesy and a thank you for our business, they upgraded us to the platinum level. We knew exactly what they were doing (we wrote the book on it!) but even so we were touched and impressed. Loews can count on us as lifelong fans for that one act of professionalism.

At the end of every ski season, our last weekend was known as "All-Star Weekend." We would invite our frequent guests back with the plan to consume all the beer and alcohol that was already open because the inn would be closed for two months. The guests would pay the full weekend rate, however the bar was free (I mean, "included" in the price.) We insisted on confiscating car keys as we were stretching the alcohol serving guidelines to their limit. Over the years, it became prestigious to get invited to All-Star Weekend. Group leaders would meet other group leaders and this wild end of season extravaganza made us more memorable in the eyes of our best customers. Even at the cost of a few brain cells.

Ramp up the Rates

Want to make some more money the easy way? Raise the rates! We don't mean to do it arbitrarily, but take a long look at your reservation book and determine whether there are weekends or weeks that you can rely on to be filled. Then it's just a matter of inching the rates northward until you meet resistance. When we bought the inn in 1986, there was one rate for all the rooms: $55 B&B for two people. It soon became clear that our weekend business was strong, while the mid-weeks tended to be a struggle. Each year we inched the rates higher, and by 1993 a standard room was $75 B&B mid-week, but the weekend 2-day (3 meals) package was $270; by 2000 the mid-week was $85 and the weekend package was up to $310.

We know quite a few innkeepers who are reluctant to increase their rates because they don't want to offend their existing customers. It was our experience that a slight bump in the rate each year was taken in stride by our regulars.

You could also explore the possibility of splitting your rooms into two or three rate levels, keeping some rooms at your current rate, and bumping the prices on your nicer rooms. You could then get a feel for how your customers react to the rate increase. I suspect that it's not a big deal because by now they're coming to you for other reasons than saving five bucks a night.

Attitude Adjustment

The Customer is Always Right

Can you live by the motto "the customer is always right?" Can you say the words "I'm sorry" even when you are quite certain that you are in the right and the guest is being unreasonable? Is it really worth winning minor skirmishes with guests and losing the war of being able to have a successful business? Smack that ego back down where it belongs. If it helps, tell yourself that you are an actor on a stage, and a successful performance (the one where your bank account gets a standing ovation) is dependent upon you satisfying every single person that walks through your front door. Your work is not over at check-in; you are still in the middle of the sales process. You want them to come back every year!

You might bristle, *"Hell no, I don't want to see these people ever again!"* Let me tell you a story that might help change your mind. Early on we had decided that we were going to be professional to *everybody* who walked through the front door. It took quite a bit of work to get them all the way to Plymouth, Vermont and we didn't want to blow it on our front door step. If we had any difficulties with a guest, we would just make a little notation on the back of the guest card to warn everybody else on the staff. We would draw a little half-moon that looked like a round of pita bread cut in half to be made into a sandwich. PITA, as in Pain In The…Astronaut.

We made it a game to try to do our very best to win over these people. Our motto was to *"Kill them with kindness!"* While it was difficult to "let these people win," a trend soon developed. You see, deep down, most people who travel to country inns are very nice people (sometimes *way* deep down). They've gone that extra mile to stay someplace special, and it's usually because they enjoy the company of other people. If they didn't, they would be staying at one of those big box motels with the word "Inn" duct taped to the end of their name.

So over the years, it turned out we developed quite the loyal following of PITA's. Well, they weren't PITA's by the time they became *returning guests*; many of them had developed into friends and loyal customers. But no matter how much you like someone, it's hard to forget your first impression. These PITA's were not used to finding love from their innkeepers because most innkeepers did not go out of their way to provide them with extraordinary customer service. It's just human nature to pull back when people are being rude to you. Our decision to double the love had to be extraordinary in the average PITA's experience, and you can be certain that they remembered to stay with us whenever they were in the area. That would be the "for better or worse" part of your innkeeping vows.

Puppy Love

Our friend Lisa would make the most extraordinary innkeeper. She greets everyone like she hasn't seen them in ages, even if she just saw you yesterday. She is just like a puppy in that regard.

What's the difference between a wife and a puppy? If you lock a puppy in your trunk for fifteen minutes, and then pop open the trunk, the puppy is still happy to see you. You'll just have to take my word on that.

Customer service is both intuitive and an art. If you don't have a natural fondness for people, you'll have your work cut out for you in this business.

So smile and be genuinely nice. And remember this old quotable from Jean Giraudoux: "The secret of success is sincerity. Once you can fake that, you've got it made."

Wedded Bliss

I also recommend that you never have a disagreement with your spouse. In thirty years of marriage, Ann and I have never had a single argument, fight or disagreement. Also, there is a really nice bridge in Brooklyn that I can get for you at an exceptional price.

It is entirely possible, nay, even likely, that you are not as blessed with an angelic, perfect, lovely, wonderful spouse as I am. You may find it more of a challenge to be on your best behavior at all times. Just remember that a guest walking through your door arrives with his own baggage, including the problems in his own life. He doesn't need your drama, and if you ever want him to walk through your door again, you won't expose him to it.

One thing that I can say with a straight face, however, is that in fifteen years of innkeeping no guest ever witnessed us "discussing our differences." We made a pact early on to hold a cease fire when we had guests in the house. This paid countless dividends over the years because it gave me time to figure out what I had done wrong before I got too heavily invested in the stupid side of the argument.

Laugh Clown, Laugh

If you really enjoy people, then innkeeping may help remedy that affliction. We've met dozens of innkeepers over the years, and one common tie that binds us is our *sense of humor*. We don't think you can get into this industry without one. Certainly you will not last for long once yours starts fraying at the edges.

What we have seen is that innkeepers who start to become burned out still have their sense of humor; they just don't display it to their guests as they once did.

You will find that you will meet all kinds of people. Eventually one of them will rub you the wrong way. Maybe you will come to not like left-handed people (or something). If you're not careful, you'll start to develop that hair trigger every time "your nemesis" checks in (*Oh crap, another southpaw*). *"Do you have left-handed spoons?"* *"Yes, they are right under the big red neon arrow pointing down to the sign that says 'left-handed spoons.' Do you have any other stupid questions?"* Arm yourself with a sense of humor, and to keep it alive you might put a sign on your bathroom mirror as I did: *ego sum usura is mirus libri* (Latin for don't let the whiners get you down.) You can see why I flunked Latin.

Miscellaneous AFTER

SOS – Save on Spending!

Although this book is focused on increasing the top line, we should pause to briefly talk about expenses. Innkeeping can be the best-ever tax shelter for the average person: deducting the music you listen to, the wine you drink, the dinners you eat at nearby restaurants, the movies you buy, your car, your insurance, and much more, offers incredible tax savings to the innkeeper. It is one of the few ways that the little guy can still catch a tax break, and as an innkeeper you can make a case for deducting just about everything that you buy with the possible exception of hair care products. Even then, if you're not too picky, with all the items left in the bathrooms you'll never have to buy shampoo again. Alriiiight – Head & Shoulders!

Don't go nuts! Just because you can *deduct* something, it doesn't mean that you should *buy* it. Talk to your accountant for his latest tax advice. Remember that commercial that began with "I'm not a doctor, but I play one on TV?" Well, I'm not an accountant; plus, they charge a heck of a lot more than this book. (Do you remember the old joke about the difference between an accountant and an actuary? They do pretty much the same thing, but the actuary lacks the accountant's cheerful and effervescent personality.)

When you buy your inn you will be tempted to make a whole bunch of changes to fine tune the inn to your personality. We encourage you to hold your financial horses. The only first year major capital expenditure we would automatically approve is for new mattresses. Except for routine maintenance and the occasional paint job, try to live with everything else for a year. There *will* come a time when your rainy day fund is going to be raided in the ugliest fashion.

In the kitchen we would switch to the best grade of coffee available. If you supply a clean room, a good night's sleep and a wonderful morning cup of Joe, you're off to a great start!

Bartering

It won't necessarily add to your top line, but may help lower your expenses if you are open to the barter system. There are magazines and online sources that can get you into barter groups. Lodging is one of the most sought after categories and you'll be amazed at some of the things that you can get for the retail cost of your room. You'll be getting $100 in goods and services for a room that would go unrented (since you're limiting the barter deal to slow times) and it will be costing you $15. Now that's leverage!

It is also pretty common to offer free (or deeply discounted) rooms to fellow innkeepers. You should arrange these visits in advance, and it will help make *your* vacationing dollar go a long way. Plus it never hurts to have another innkeeper speaking fondly of your property!

Between the Sheets

My mom used to say, "House work is horse work," and this goes double for doing the laundry for an inn full of guests. We were able to rent crisp white sheets, towels and tablecloths from People's Linen, a wonderful company that offered their services all over the area in Vermont and New Hampshire. If at all possible, rent your linens. When they're dirty, you toss them into the magic hamper and fresh clean ones appear the next day in your linen closet. To this day we still get a laugh with innkeeper friends John and Debbie, then owners of the *Depot Corner Inn* in Ludlow, Vermont, who burned through a couple of irons in their first few weeks before they learned about linen rental.

As a side bonus, your linen truck driver has his finger on the pulse of almost every property in town, and you can get a good sense of the business climate by chatting with him.

Advertising Dollars and Sense

Your new advertising guiding principle should be: "If it's free, it's for me." Try to get into other people's webpages, guidebooks, seasonal publications, monthly magazines and newspapers, and in that order. You want to be in any publication that you can – more is better – and the longer the shelf life the better, especially if you're paying for it.

Your goal with any advertising is to get the traveling public to give you a second look. Sure, you want an actual reservation, but it is more likely that you'll only get someone's interest piqued to either call you or go to your webpage. Be ready! Have an over-the-top bananas *I must see this place* webpage ready and waiting for them on the internet. There are untold resources out there on how to produce a webpage. You don't have to be the talent, you just need to write the check and have it done.

Leverage the power of the internet. You know that you have a wonderful product to sell, and you only need a dozen people to find you every day. When someone is web searching for lodging in your area, you want to come up near the top of the first page.

One funny story comes to mind. We noticed that there were a lot of beer drinkers coming to the area, so we tailored part of our webpage to target them. Vermont has more breweries per capita than any state in the union. That may sound impressive, but it's really just because

Vermont has very few capita. (They have mostly cows, and they're on the wagon.)

At the other end of our road was a brewery that was just starting out, called the Long Trail Brewery. They brewed the delicious Long Trail Ale, and we were proud to be the first establishment to put them on tap. One of their managers contacted us one day to complain that when people searched for *their* brewery on the internet, *our inn* would always come up before their name on the web searches. He wanted us to put a stop to that!

Other than being at a loss for words since we could not tell the search engines in what order to produce results, we were secretly pleased to be coming in ahead of the brewery when people were actually searching for *their* beer. We weren't going to make a ton of money selling their beer at our pub, but we were certainly likely to get an overnight room if someone wanted to come up to Vermont for a brewery tour.

Make sure that your online brochure (webpage) is written with well thought out *keywords*. There are techniques that can move you up the Google, Bing and other search engines' priority lists (including *paid* techniques) to optimize your exposure. Talk to your techie about SEO (Search Engine Optimization). Just don't get the beer guy too angry.

For newspapers and magazines, have a digital and physical press package ready to go. Include photographs and complete descriptions of your rooms that anyone is free to publish.

Daily newspapers are not right for your advertising dollar. I can't think of anything with a shorter shelf life except maybe a radio ad or a mosquito's honeymoon.

Before we became busy with the bike tour business, we placed only one regular paid advertisement each year. We bought a half-page ad on the back cover of the Summer Issue of the Vermont Chamber of Commerce Travel Guide. It was a fancy "coffee table" type of magazine that people would use all summer long. More importantly, it was so nice that people would save this magazine and use it year after year as a Vermont traveling reference. Now that's a long magazine shelf life!

Marketing Blunder of the Century?

One television show that we really enjoyed back during our innkeeping days was Bob Newhart running his Vermont country inn. It was great publicity at the time to get people into Vermont to see what the country inn lifestyle was all about. As funny as the show was, it had absolutely nothing to do with the reality of running a Vermont inn. Bob's weekly antics usually revolved around the town and the staff and only occasionally involved actual paying guests checking into his Stratford Inn. (*Sooo* close to our last name, it was like we missed winning the lottery by one number.) Local backwoodsmen Larry, Darryl and Darryl were hilarious, but they did not help pay the bills.

The inn that was used for the outside establishing shots for the Newhart show made the marketing blunder of the century (in our humble opinion). After the show started airing, they repainted the exterior of the inn in a completely different color scheme – from white to brown! If we were advising them (even today) we would make sure that their inn now and forever looks EXACTLY like the inn shown at the beginning of the Newhart show (down to the size of the bushes.) That is unique marketing that an inn of their size could never afford. I would also stuff Bob Newhart and put him on the front lawn. What's that? Oh. He's not? Never mind.

(As of today, Bob is 83 years young, and still one of the world's funniest men. That's my lame attempt at flattery by imitation of Bob's hilarious comedy bits when he talks into the phone and you can't hear the other guy speaking. What's that? Day job? Right.)

The Guidebooks

Get listed in as many *free* guide books as possible. I emphasize free, because there are quite a few out there where the publication requires you to buy your listing. In our experience, these publications tend to end up being more self-serving than effective. Those guidebooks that sell on the strength of the inns that they select gain a better reputation for honesty, and therefore are used much more often by the traveling public. You need to meet their criteria before they will devote their precious book space to you.

If you can pay to be in a guidebook, then anyone can pay to be on the pages before and after you. The guidebooks that are less picky about their inns don't sell as well. As Groucho Marx once said, "Please accept my resignation. I don't want to belong to any club that will accept me as a member."

Two of the national ratings guidebook companies will automatically come to you if you ask them: AAA and Mobil (although, why people will take advice from a gas station as to where they should eat and sleep has always bugged me). Of these ratings companies, AAA brought us the most business.

The single exception to the rule of not paying to be in Guidebooks is AAA. They will charge you $200-$400 for your application and inspection, but we think that the business they bring over the years is worth the investment. Be ready for your first inspection, because if you are not satisfied with the rating and you ask for another inspection, you will have to pay another fee.

Now it is time to order that case of plastic-wrapped cups for the bathrooms. We fought this for years thinking it was just not quaint, but that was before we discovered the secret to improving your AAA rating. They will send an inspector to your property who will tour the guest bedrooms before finally making "the big decision" as to your diamond rating.

The AAA inspector has a certain degree of flexibility in his rating. He also has a clipboard with dozens of little places to make check marks on the items that you have in your rooms. Your goal is to befriend the inspector and give him a reason to bump you into the next highest category. Since you are already a charming innkeeper and are being nice to everyone who comes through the door, this should not require any extra effort.

You need the master list of what AAA requires its inspectors to look for in a guest bedroom. At first you will see this list and think, well it's nice, but we already have a lot of this stuff. Your goal is to have as much of this stuff as humanly possible. Many items are small things that you can do for less than $100 per room.

Before you schedule your AAA inspection, Google *"AAA Approval Requirements and Diamond rating Guidelines"* to find the current list of room (and facility) amenities that they look for. Some of the silly stuff (to us) included *wrapped* paper cups, *8 matching* hangers (10 hangars for 4-diamond; 2 of which are satin), and *two* bars of soap (sizes specified to the ¼ ounce). We suppose that these are all pretty good ideas, but up to now you might not have focused on the amenities conforming from room to room.

By completing all the items on the checklist, you have given the inspector some legitimate reasons to bump you up to the next category. In my opinion, our inn, being older and shall we say "less fancy," should have been rated two diamonds. But that second time we asked AAA to come through, we hit it off with the inspector (who had the requisite checklist and clipboard) and low and behold the check marks were flying onto the paper as fast as he could confirm them.

We made it easy for the inspector to justify a three diamond rating, which we enjoyed for the last ten years. So were we really a two-diamond inn with a three-diamond rating? I didn't think so! What we might have lacked in the physical property, we made up in the intangible department. If you give your guest five-diamond friendliness, then they will never complain to AAA about your three-diamond rating!

Also, the pet traveling public often has a challenge finding pet-friendly country inns. Try to get in these pet guidebooks if your inn qualifies. We saw them being used all the time.

Monogrammed Shirts and Souvenirs

We still remember a story from our first summer of innkeeping. We had a visit from one fellow who must have been brought up in a bazaar bargaining for everything he ever purchased in life. He and his (long suffering, I would guess) wife were "just driving by" and if we could see our way clear to letting them stay for half of the room rate, then they would agree to stay with us.

We asked him what their plans were and he said that they were just driving around and exploring the area. They had no set itinerary and could just as easily *not* spend the night with us. We were standing in the front hallway during this discussion, and he had not even seen the guest bedrooms. He wanted the discount even *before* he knew what we had to offer.

Well, we were empty that night, so we made him a deal. We said if he spent the night with us he could have tomorrow at half-rate, *but only if he decided that he didn't like the place*. If he liked it, he would have to pay the full rate. We don't think we necessarily bent over backwards for these folks, as we were rookie innkeepers and everybody was getting the full-on love treatment anyway, but when it came time to check out, he insisted on paying the full rate for both nights! We (being rookies) were insisting that we wanted to give him half-off on the second night anyway.

We compromised and they left with smiles, having paid the full rate but getting two inn shirts as souvenirs (costing us $10). When they arrived *for a week* the next summer, they couldn't wait to show up together at the check-in desk proudly wearing their matching inn shirts.

It was around then we decided that each year we would produce a *different* colored shirt for each calendar year. Collect the set! Did you get your dark blue one?

Some years later, one guest "just had to call" from New York City when she saw another person in an elevator wearing one of our inn shirts. She instantly started up a conversation with this fellow (you know how New Yorkers love to chat with each other in elevators) and they reminisced about the inn. We had made it a point to invest in the best quality shirts possible (so that people would wear them and that they would last a long time) and to sell them at bargain prices. They were walking advertising.

Everybody Loves Love

Make it a point to use the word "love." People love "love." What's not to like about "love." (Facebook needs a "Love" button, because you can't click "Like" twice.) You never say that you *don't mind* making arrangements for guests. You don't say you'll do it for them *if they want you to*. You are showing enthusiasm and telling them that you *love* them. If you can't be nice, then hire someone who can be.

And while we're on the subject, never, ever say the words *"No problem"* to a guest's request. Train your staff never to say those horrible words. *Of course* a guest's request is *"No problem!"* Your answer to a guest's request will always be that *you would love to do it*, or *you would be happy to do it*. And since variety is the spice of life, you can also say it would *be your pleasure* or you would *be pleased to do it*. You got a problem with that?

Gift Certificate Success

Everybody wants to sell gift certificates because it's like selling a room without having to clean the toilet.

Here's an idea for your consideration: take your gift certificate program to the next level. Every inn should have them and offer them on their webpage. They can either be automatic (print at home) or you could guarantee overnight delivery for last minute gift ideas. Make sure you advertise this to everybody who comes in the door or visits your webpage.

You're going to take your gift certificate program to yet another level. You are going to give them to people who canceled their reservation even after they canceled within your *strict* cancellation period! So yes, you are going to take their money. Your cancellation policy is tough, but it is coated in sugar. The next day you are going to send them a Gift Certificate in the full amount of their "lost" deposit telling them that you are sorry that they missed you. (It is like the old joke where one polar bear is explaining to the other polar bear about igloos. He points to one and says, "They're crunchy on the outside and chewy on the inside." OK, not the perfect analogy, but I like the visual!)

We used to joke that the *easiest guest* was the one who paid and never showed up. That may be true in the short run, but you lose out on the chance for a repeat customer if they lose money and have a bad taste in their mouth because of it.

The happy medium that we found was to give them a gift certificate in the full amount of their lost deposit, but with one stipulation: it could only be used during the non-holiday mid-weeks, and it had to be used within one year. It was like giving them their money back, saying "come back, all is forgiven; we still love you!"

What have you done here? You have pocketed $100 for the deposit, and only given back the $15 cost of the room, should they ever use it. It was our experience that when they came back was not just for one night. They would feel semi-obligated to spend more time with you because you did them a favor in the first place.

If they don't use the gift certificate within a year, they were probably not going to be regular customers anyway. But that's only probably. Not certainly, so don't give up on them yet. For "expired" gift certificates we would allow them to apply the full amount to a mid-week stay, for up to 50% of their bill. It is still a win-win, and you keep the hope alive that they will someday get through the front door and you can wow them with a great customer experience. We had quite a few guests who took a long time to finally visit us. Once they did, several put us on their annual itineraries.

Incidentally, we never did have much luck when we gave away a bedroom to a charity. It would usually end up in the hands of somebody who would not necessarily choose us as a place to vacation, and we might not have been exactly what they expected. We're not saying don't give away your rooms to a good cause, but you might want to limit it to a time when the room would not be filled anyway.

Damn Quaint

Our experience with "charity" gift certificates did highlight how much our webpage served to effectively filter out people ill-suited to us. In fact, the second line on our webpage after the name of the inn was "*Damn Quaint*." That alone screened the people who were expecting the Ritz Carlton. It told the traveler that we didn't take ourselves too seriously and that he could probably have some fun at our place.

We had some fun with our "*Damn Quaint*" tag line when we tried to place an advertisement in *Yankee Magazine*. Their sales representative called and said that they refused to print the word "*Damn*." After some negotiations, we were able to get them to agree to mostly scratching out the word "*Damn*" and inserting a hand-drawn "*Darn*" with a carat. Does this sound familiar? We use this "carat technique" on the cover of *this* book. It was an eye catcher, and many people told us that the phrase got them interested enough to read just a little more of our webpage.

My other book, *How I Wrote TWO eBooks in 21 Days* uses both the "carat technique" *and* the catch phrase *"Damn Funny!"* Nope, this is not a coincidence.

Give Me a Break!

One of the things that you will discover is that as charming as your location is, even *it* will begin to get old after a while. We lived in a gorgeous valley in the Green Mountains, one-third of the way up the state and smack dab in the middle. We could step outside and see stunning views up to the mountains in all directions. What's not to like, right?

We were smart. Or lucky, which is probably better. We learned the burnout lessons early, so our mental toast was never blackened to the point we couldn't serve it. Rejuvenation breaks allowed us to greet all the guests with the enthusiasm that they deserved.

For the Vermont innkeeper, there are two natural lulls in the working year. There are five or six weeks after the fall foliage has been raked into piles but before the winter snow arrives for ski season. It's gray and cold, and nobody really wants to be there. Innkeepers, spent from the foliage crush, are girding their loins for ski season, so it's a great time to take a little break to unwind. Your loins will thank you.

After the winter, there's another break. Northern New England has five seasons: spring, summer, fall, winter and mud. This last one comes while the final vestiges of snow are melting, but before it is time to mow the lawn, usually from late March until early May. So enjoy those naturally occurring vacation breaks during slow times because you've earned them!

Expanding

Is there any way that you can expand your property? There's a great story about a famous hotelier who would give up his room and sleep in a closet in order to sell one last room (his own!) That kind of dedication seemed to have worked out pretty well for Mr. Hilton.

It stands to reason that if *THE BREAD IS IN THE BED*, the more beds that you have, the more bread you make. But first you need to look more closely at the occupancy history. To illustrate, let me tell you our story.

When we bought the Salt Ash Inn, it was easy enough to open the bedrooms of the previous innkeepers' kids to the public, and we had (at no additional expense) an instant two more guest bedrooms! More beds, more heads, more bread. Once we had a handle on what we could expect in reservations, we had to decide if we wanted to spend the money to invest in *even more* guest bedrooms. There was a concrete foundation on the property where a carriage house once stood, and for years it was crying out to be rebuilt into guest bedrooms.

When it comes to deciding about expanding your property, you will probably have to speak with a representative of the banking community. Bankers are a necessary evil. Mark Twain said that there are three kinds of lies: lies, damn lies and statistics. When you approach banks for a loan, you'll find that their understanding of the hospitality business begins and ends with *one number*: your annual occupancy rate.

Ours was around 25%. Pretty lousy, right? Not so fast! Does 25% mean that on every single night of the year three quarters of the inn was empty? Who knows? You need to look much more closely at the reservation history, and then *patiently* explain it to your banker.

If you were in downtown Lahaina, Maui (a year round tourist destination) and had only 25% occupancy every night, then there is a problem. But if you are seasonal with monstrously strong bookings when the doors are open, it sheds a whole new light on the 25% figure. If you truly only fill one quarter of the inn every night of the year, it makes no sense to build another room. If you find that you're turning away people every single weekend, the property may be perfect for expansion.

We had *at least* 48 nights each year where we could have filled the inn two times over (12 winter weekends, 2 holiday weeks and 14 foliage nights). Even at our standard rate, these nights would make expansion profitable. That we ended up charging deluxe rates for these beautiful rooms only made them more lucrative.

So imagine my surprise when I checked the webpage of our old inn and noticed that one of the bedrooms had been turned into a sitting room! Sure, it's a great place for congregating (it *was* the former town Post Office!) but it was *much* more profitable as a bedroom. Sure, it was usually one of the last bedrooms that we would ever rent because it is located next to the bar. It was one of our "economy" rooms, and we charged a little less to be in this room because of the evening revelry. But the room is adjacent to an outside door, which made it a good candidate for "pet friendly." And with 48 guaranteed room nights each year, it's a pretty expensive sitting room. It will make a good candidate to turn back into a guest room someday.

One last thing to remember about statistics: 82.76% of them are made up.

Sleep Around

In *The Sound of Music* the Mother Abbess sings *"Climb every mountain; Ford every stream; Follow every rainbow, Till you find your dream."* I'm pretty sure she skipped the verse that says *"Sleep in every guest room; Use every shower; Eat your own damn breakfast; Till you find your flaws!"* My songwriting career might not take off any time soon, but the advice is still "sound."

Stay in every room for a few nights. Pack a suitcase and try to live as a guest would. Not only does it add variety to your life, but you'll unearth any "room challenges" before too many guests do. A satisfied guest is a potential returning customer.

Selling – Hey Wait, I Just Got Here!

It is said in the boating world that the two happiest days of a boat owner's life are the day he buys his boat and the day he sells it. (Note to self: don't buy a boat.)

Having been through both the buying and selling processes, we can tell you that holds true for the innkeeper! As thrilled as you are to begin your new career on day one, you are just as thrilled to leave it in your rearview mirror when the time comes. We enjoyed the heck out of our decade and a half of innkeeping, but when it became time to leave it felt like we had one foot out the door and the other one stapled to the brochure rack. It's not that we were completely burnt-out on innkeeping; it just got to the point that we were more excited to move on to our next adventure.

Honest Dividends

You will find that many times travelers will pay their bills in cash. Now we don't want to preach about honesty being the best policy, but it will pay off when it comes time to sell your inn. A mere mortal might be tempted to stick a little cash in his sock and not have it ever reach the books. We urge you never to give in to this temptation.

Every year we joked that *this* would be the year that we were going to cheat on the taxes, but we never did quite get around to it. This paid off when we sold the inn as our revenues supported the sales price.

The sales price of your property is significantly dependent upon the income that it has generated in its operation. The price that one pays for an inn will need to be supported by the profits that the inn generates as a going concern. There are other things that go into the sales price of an inn, but you will get more money for your property when you are able to show strong and consistent earnings statements. You will need your records to support the sales price that you deserve.

Depreciation is Depressing

When you are first starting out it is not likely that you'll have huge profits to worry about. It is entirely possible that you will be in a tax bracket well below the highest level. You won't exactly be in the Occupy Movement, but you *are* in the 99%. Guess what (probably) happens on the day that you sell the inn? According to Uncle Sam, *you are rich - congratulations!* It may not feel like it, but since you have depreciated your property substantially, you will have a whopper of a capital gains tax bill, very likely in the highest tax bracket.

As far as the tax man is concerned, you are *Queen for a day.* I don't want to get too political, but with our gangs of elected Robin Hoods in Washington it is becoming quite popular to "soak the rich" to pay for their overspending. I don't think it takes too much of a crystal ball to see that this could get more challenging for the higher income brackets.

So throughout your innkeeping years, it might be prudent to keep your taxable "basis" higher by not depreciating the physical property. Don't be penny wise and pound foolish. You might pay a little more in taxes each year, but it will be in the lower tax bracket while you are still "poor."

On the other hand, you may think that taxes are headed down, in which case you should take advantage of all the tax breaks that you can get. At least you will be making your depreciation decisions knowing the possible consequences. Not many innkeepers consider the tax implications of *selling* before they *buy*, but they should. Consult with your friendly personable accountant on this.

Just Say No to Notes

The buyer might want you to finance a part of the transaction. I urge you to do everything you can to avoid this. When you walk away, you would like to do it cleanly. If you absolutely must take back a second mortgage, don't count on it for your retirement plan. It is entirely possible that the new innkeepers coming in will not be as good as you were and the business may suffer a hiccup. If they are not well capitalized to weather this hiccup (and that's possible since they're asking *you* to help finance them) then you could end up being paid nothing when the bank forecloses on them (you will be in a second position behind the bank.)

If push comes to shove and you simply *must* take back a second mortgage to make the transaction happen, make it as unappealing to the buyer as possible (and tell him why you are doing it.) Put a higher interest rate on the note, even if you write it for a little less money. You want them to be eager to pay off your loan as soon as possible. At least you'll get a big return on the money before they stop paying you altogether.

Get Involved Finding a Buyer

When we listed with a broker to sell the inn, we reserved the right to sell directly to any buyers that we found on our own. It just rubbed us the wrong way that we had been working our tail feathers off for 15 years and an inn broker would be getting 10% of our sales price just to find us a buyer. We know this opens the door for a whole other discussion, but our point here is that there are things that *you* can do to find a buyer.

We registered the domain name countryinnforsale.com and put a complete buyer's package (except finances) on the internet. This turned out to be the connection that brought our buyer to us, and we completed the sale without the assistance of a broker. (You could Google the "wayback machine" and still find our old selling webpage from 1999. We noticed that the domain name was used again in 2006 and 2011, and is currently for *lease* to the next person who wants to use it. Now why didn't we think of that?)

You will have quite a few guests through the years who will show real interest in becoming innkeepers. Keep a file on the side with their contact information. You could send them a note (if you're not trying to keep it a secret) asking if they or anybody they know might be interested in purchasing your inn. Don't let all that good sales training go to waste!

CAVEAT EMPTOR –
War Stories from Innkeeping Hell

The innkeepers in our association used to have a gentleman's agreement (*only half joking*) that no one was allowed to write "the book" until everyone in the association sold. You weren't allowed to ruin it for the next guy who wanted to get out of the business.

It reminds me of the old story where the carnival comes to town and sets up a tent with a huge sign that says, *"Come see the horse with a head where his tail ought to be!"* People pay the barker a nickel and walk into the tent (okay, it's an *old* story) then leave out the back smiling, shaking their heads and looking chagrined. As it turns out, it was just a regular horse; but he was standing backwards in the stall. Similarly, no innkeeper was allowed to write "the book" so as to prevent the next prospective innkeeper/sucker from coming along and paying the nickel to learn the hard way about being taken to the cleaners. We all must keep the innkeeping fantasy alive!

These are the things that your friendly innkeepers are talking about at their meetings. We found it kind of comforting to know that we all felt like we were in the same leaky boat.

Aw, Crap

You will get to know and love every toilet in your house. As nice as you are to them, as shiny as you make them, as sweetly as you talk to them, someday, somehow they are going to misbehave. I am (affectionately, I hope) known by Ann as "Toilet Man!" Whenever she would say, "Hey, Toilet Man," I knew I didn't want to hear the rest of the sentence.

We had twenty toilets in the house, and I was buddies with each one. They all had their personalities, and needed love and attention in different ways. This alone should be good reason not to ever become an innkeeper. I have logged many commode repair hours in my life that I will never get back.

Usually it was no problem, and Toilet Man could take care of it with technique perfected through the years. But every once in a while: *Katie bar the door!*

If there were children in the room, I had a hint of what the problem might be. If there was a baby, look for mom trying to flush a "disposable" diaper the size of Rhode Island. If it was a preschooler, all bets were off. I would have to remove the toilet, walk it down to the driveway and dump it upside down to see what treasure the little angel tried to flush.

Two different times someone tried to flush a toothbrush, and I can almost understand that. Almost. I mean, who

wants to reach in and pull a toothbrush out of the toilet?
You're never going to use it again anyway!

The most bizarre item that I ever dumped out of a toilet
was a night light. And there were only adults staying in
the room. What kind of moron would think you could
flush a night light? Like they didn't see it tumble in? Feel
the splash? What were they trying to illuminate anyway?
Some people are just not very bright.

Hey, Toilet Man!

There is a pleasant little expression that says the roof doesn't leak when the sun is shining. The more menacing (to an innkeeper) expression might be "your septic field won't crap out with just a few guests in the house."

We were somewhat victimized by our own success when business started to boom. At the end of one Presidents' Day weekend, the septic field decided that it was tired, thank you very much, and that it was going on its own vacation.

The tip of the iceberg was when Ann called me over and said, "Hey, Toilet Man." My first thought was, "Here we go again;" I was much too busy to unclog another toilet. But I gathered my tools of the trade: bucket, plunger, rubber gloves, towels and *steely resolve* and headed for the first floor bedroom having the "plumbing challenge."

As I did my thing, and made nice-nice to the commode, I soon realized that this had become a "stage two plumbing challenge." My usual ministrations had no effect, and I was going to have to remove the toilet to look for toothbrushes and night lights.

Looking back, I would have sold my soul if all I needed to do was scrap another night light.

"New and different" oftentimes translated to "fun and interesting," but alas not that time. When I removed the toilet (after I scooped out the bowl contents one…stinky…cup…at a time) I discovered that the entire pipe was filled to the brim with, *umm, "effluent."*

It was about that time when Ann poked her head into the bathroom and said "Hey, Toilet Man." It was unusual for her to nag me (honest!) about finishing a job while I was still clearly working on it, so I suspected that she has left her blueberry pancake station just to say "hi" and see how I was doing. No such luck. She had come to tell me that two other rooms on the first floor also needed their toilets (and showers) unclogged. I might have been born at night, but it wasn't *last* night, and my pulse began to race.

It was in the middle of February, the filet mignon of the winter, and we had thirty guests checking-in and a septic system checking-out. My brain began to rapid fire through the "what's the worst that could happen?" possibilities and I realized that we were going to lose a bundle of money when we sent our hard won guests to nearby properties. A microsecond later I realized that it was next to impossible to find fourteen bedrooms within a 100-mile radius of us. It was President's Week for goodness sakes!

In desperation I called every honey dipper in the phone book. I finally found a septic guy who came to do an emergency pump-out of our 2,500 gallon holding tank. His name was Goodwin, and he arrived within the hour. I immediately liked him because on his pump-out truck was a cartoon drawing of a toilet and an oversized TP roll with the pithy caption: "No job is finished until the paperwork is done!"

We had a scavenger hunt for the top of the holding tank, which had remained unopened in our tenure (at least up to this point). The former innkeepers had given us a treasure map that showed where the top of the tank should have been, but we couldn't seem to locate the map. Maybe we needed a map to the map? Fortunately, Don and Ginny were still in town (they had built a home nearby and were focusing on their local business) and Don came right over and helped us locate the tank.

In short order we filled the septic truck and I breathed a sigh of relief. It didn't last long though, because Ann soon poked her head out and said "Hey, Toilet Man." I figured she was asking for an update, but again, no such luck. We now had a *second* floor room with a clog; the first-floor rooms had long since been unavailable for flushing and brushing.

It turned out that while we may have had thousands of gallons of new capacity in the front lawn, the poop in the pipes hadn't gotten the memo and was stubbornly parked in said pipes awaiting an engraved invitation to flow outside to the empty tank.

These pipes were going to need a couple more hours of coaxing, begging and pleading to flow again. The departing guests were sympathetic, and they wished us well at check-out before they scurried off to find a bathroom.

Between a long metal snake and some ingenuity with an air compressor, we finally restored order, and everything worked by late afternoon. All fourteen rooms were changing over, and the new guests who were coming in for five nights didn't suspect a thing. I waved goodbye to Goodwin, and thanked him for being available. If I wasn't so focused on the inn, I would have arranged to meet him in a social setting because he was that friendly. I made a mental note to call him in a few weeks and offer to buy him a beer.

First we needed to regroup and get back into the swing of things. It was not that easy as my adrenaline had been pumping all day long.

We always tried to behave as consummate professionals, and the week started smoothly. We were the calm duck on the serene pond: to the naked eye, we were cool, calm and collected, but below the surface we were paddling like crazy trying to maintain sanity. Ever so slowly, the "septic challenge" panic began to lessen.

But Tuesday morning while I was still in bed (I was the late shift at the pub; Ann was the early shift at the stove.) Ann poked her head into the room and woke me with a loving, "Hey, Toilet Man." As there was no rest for the weary, I gathered the accoutrements and headed down to the first floor bathroom that started this whole thing to see what was wrong this time.

Sure enough, the pipes were filled again. And just as it did two days before, my pulse started to race. I knew for a fact that there was plenty of room in the holding tank, and I knew for a fact that the pipes were clear because we had spent hours flushing them. The only thing this could have meant was that the entire leach field was clogged and needed to be cleaned or replaced.

Clearly the universe wanted me to make friends with Goodwin, so I called him and told him my latest challenge. He was appropriately sympathetic (we were buddies now) and he came over to pump out the holding tank. This was to be the beginning of a long and prosperous (for him) business relationship. We were in the middle of the winter and our holding tank was going to need to be emptied every few days.

For six weeks we sat on pins and needles, and listening to someone take a five-minute shower was like watching the gas pump numbers spin like helicopter blades. This duck might have been a serene bird on the outside, but below the surface I was in full blown panic mode. My alarm manifested itself in hand-written signs that sprouted like spring flowers, and asked people to please, *please* limit their showering, flushing and brushing. These were not my finest make-the-guest-feel-comfortable moments.

Time marched on, and somehow we made it through the season. To his credit, even though he had us over a smelly barrel, Goodwin cut us a financial break on the multiple pump outs. And I must say that he looked quite dashing in his new Corvette.

Field of Dreams

The only good news about the dead septic field was that the inn was now officially closed for mud season. The bad news was that if we didn't want to spend the entire summer working to put Goodwin's kids through college, we were going to have to figure out what to do with the septic system.

We called the local jack-of-all-trades contractor, who had equipment right in town. As a savvy business person, he knew that our options were limited, and (I thought) priced his quote to replace our septic field accordingly. Through the years we would come to know Billy much better, and with 20/20 hindsight I know that my thinking was wrong. He was as honest as the day is long.

Our emergency fund was raided by the deer rampage (that story is coming shortly – trust me) and Goodwin's new wheels, and in any case could not have funded a new $50k septic field. So we headed off to the bank, hat in hand, and looked for a loan to help us stay in business.

I won't say that the bankers were difficult to work with, and many of them probably didn't actually drown puppies for fun, but working with them was quite frustrating. To me it was an easy call. They had our mortgage and we would soon not be paying it at all unless they ponied up $50k more.

At this point you probably have a pretty good idea of how I operated. My mom used to say about me, *"Give him an inch and he'll take a mile. "* So once the bank agreed to give us the money, I hit them up for another $50k so we could build the carriage house on that forlorn foundation out back and put in four more bedrooms. We were able to show them a few years of completely booked weekends, and made a pretty good case that we would be able to pay off the additional loan.

Forgiveness, not Permission

One of the benefits of dealing with a local contractor is his ability to get things done politically. Billy was on the town zoning board and therefore was able to get his bulldozer to our front lawn within the week.

All was going swimmingly until a state inspector knocked on our front door and asked what we were doing on the front lawn. I explained that we needed emergency repairs to our septic system. He understood completely and then asked to see our permit. Our what? You know, the *permit* from the state that says you can make repairs to your septic system? (Oh *that* permit; it must be in my other pants.)

I was under the impression that you did not need a permit if you were only making repairs, and that permits were only required for *new* construction. I did not know that for a *fact*, and preferred to remain blissfully ignorant instead of asking too many questions. I figured if Billy was willing to dig, then I was willing to let him.

The whole project came to a screeching halt while we prepared an emergency application for the state septic field permit. I suppose the inspector could have been harder on us, and he did turn out to be quasi-helpful by expediting the approvals process. But he would have been *more* helpful if he had just driven past our property and ignored the bulldozer.

Unfortunately, he told us that the new carriage house would have to have its own independent holding tank and leach field. We could not tie it into the inn septic system as we had planned. The only area for a leach field was on the front lawn next to the existing leach field, and we were going to have to dig a long trench from the Carriage House through the woods to the front lawn.

But first, we had to figure out where our property line was. You might think it odd that we did not already know our property boundaries, but in Vermont it was not too unusual to see lot descriptions that are vague. They'll say something like "from the tree that looks like a bear, continuing along a stone wall and then in a general Northeasterly direction to the rock that cousin Elmer skinned his knee on." I suspect that in 100 years, lot lines will be GPS mapped down to the millimeter, but these land descriptions were written in more gentlemanly times.

And hey, what's another expense for professional services when we're spending money like sailors on shore leave? So we hired a surveyor to put stakes in the ground to make sure we didn't tear up any woods on the next-door neighbor's property.

At long last, we started to make progress again. The bulldozer on the front lawn was fired up and a backhoe was brought in to dig the trench for the new septic line.

There is a certain road that is paved with good intentions and leads to an extremely warm climate. While digging our trench, unbeknownst to us, we were traveling the on-ramp to this road. Our next door neighbor had decided that one (*small*) section of our trench was a couple of feet over what he believed to be the property line *in the woods*. We showed him our recent survey and said that we were quite certain that we were well within our side of the line. And in any case, what's the big deal? We're only talking about maybe a 10 foot section, 2-3 feet away from where he thought the line should be *in the woods*.

We proceeded with the construction, opened the new bedrooms and began to get settled into an innkeeping routine. Could we now, finally, get back to what we came to Vermont in the first place to do - keep an inn? What do you think?

Not Guilty, Your Honor

One night *when we were serving dinner*, a police officer
came to the door and asked us to step into another room.
He said that he had come to serve court papers. We were
being sued by our next-door neighbor. This was really
not what we had signed up for; we had just wanted to
meet people, flip pancakes, and enjoy the beautiful
Vermont scenery.

We were being sued for big bucks for something like
"unjust enrichment," which basically said that the only
reason we had made money in the new building was
because we had stolen land from the next door neighbor.
It of course had nothing to do with the blood, sweat and
tears that we had put into our business; we would not
have made that money if we weren't thieves.

This was now the second time we had been sued as
innkeepers. The first was a slip-and-fall where a guest
apparently did not understand that it might not have been
prudent to walk out in the snow in her open Dr. Scholl's
sandals. Clearly it was our fault for not telling her, and
our insurance company paid her a few thousand dollars
to, shall we say, *walk* away.

This time we did not get off so cheaply. We were taken
all the way to a jury trial. And really, was there any doubt
in the first place that we would not have been able to
come to a reasonable solution before we involved the
court system? Everybody looked at businesses with

dollar signs in their eyes, and you couldn't swing a dead cat without hitting a lawyer that would take a case on contingency.

Now we had legal expenses that were starting to mount, and on the advice of our lawyer we (very reluctantly) sued Steve, our surveyor friend, for negligence. We really liked Steve, but our lawyer explained to us that if the jury found for the complainant, then we could have been liable for not only the profits that we made in the new building but a multiple of them as a penalty. We needed some deep pockets behind us in case the survey was wrong, and that was why surveyors carried insurance, right?

Now we'd dragged Steve into our drama, and *his* legal expenses were beginning. By the time our court date rolled around, the only happy people in the room were the lawyers. It reminded me of the old joke about the town that was too small to support a lawyer. Then a second lawyer moved to town and there was plenty of work for the both of them.

In one of those dramatic trial day negotiations that we had previously only seen on TV, the neighbor's lawyer said that they were dropping the "unjust enrichment" part of the suit, and they would only be asking the court make us move the septic pipe and to pay reasonable legal fees. So we made a deal to drop our suit against Steve if he agreed to move the pipe at no cost to us should we lose.

As a bad workman blames his tools, I blamed our lawyer for losing our case. Or maybe that's not fair, and he was just out-lawyered by the other team. We only had facts and logic on our side. As it turns out, they had really cool displays and diagrams. Even I was impressed, and would have been inclined to go with the complainant had I not known just how ridiculous their case was.

Dropping the "unjust enrichment" turned out to be a pretty smooth move on their part. They went from being gold diggers to just being victims in a heartbeat. The jury only saw a poor little Vermonter being bullied by the big bad business next door. These kindly people only wanted the big bad business to move its unlawfully-located septic pipe and to pay the legal expenses that they were forced to incur to defend their God-given property rights. Was that too much to ask? You could almost picture the little orphan in _Oliver_ holding up his porridge bowl asking in a pitiful voice, *"Please sir, may I have another?"*

As I say, we lost the lawsuit. Steve lived up to his end of the bargain and moved the pipe on his own dime. If I remember correctly, we ponied up about $20 grand to pay their "reasonable" legal fees.

Are you sure that you still want to be an innkeeper?

By the Skin of our Teeth

Or maybe I should say, by the skin of the dog's teeth.
Our old yellow Lab Brandy adapted to the inn life quite
easily. I think becoming an inn dog is akin to winning the
doggie lottery. Once you get petted by 1,000 people
every year, you tend to get a little spoiled.

One night in the pub, a guest thought it would be
entertaining to bring out his pet cockatiel. I'm not sure
what possessed him to do it, but he thought it would be
fun if he let it fly around the pub. I can tell you that
Brandy sure thought it was exciting!

Sitting comfortably under some guest's ministrations,
Brandy caught sight of the bird through half-open eyes.
She took off like a shot (who knew the old girl had it in
her?) and in five steps snagged the bird out of midair and
brought it to me behind the bar with the biggest butt wag
that I had seen in years.

All's well that ends well, and Brandy released the bird
unharmed from her soft Labrador mouth. I think she
wanted me to throw it again so she could fetch. The
whole thing happened so quickly that the bird owner
wasn't able to utter much more than a squeak (he kind of
sounded like his bird).

When I handed the bird back to him he looked it over and
quickly put it back in its cage (where it belonged). It
doesn't bear to think too much about what could have

gone wrong with this situation. If you haven't figured it out by now, this innkeeping thing is for the birds.

Keep Calm and Carry On

The fire looked like a massive blowtorch coming out of the furnace. It was Sunday morning breakfast when Ann smelled something burning and looked around to find the source. After one glance in the basement, she hurried to me in the pub where I was checking-out a guest. She used *the special spouse communication tone* when she asked, "Honey, can you come here now?" I dropped everything to follow her, but she was already halfway to the kitchen.

One look down the basement door and I could see yellow light flickering on the walls, but not too much smoke. I told her to call the fire department while I took a closer look. The back of the furnace looked like a flame thrower!

Lucky for us, it was only firing against the stone foundation. There was an emergency shutoff switch at the head of the stairs, and this turned off the flame thrower instantly. Nothing had caught fire, so we called the FD and told them that the immediate emergency was over, and they could come at their leisure.

We made a brief announcement to the dining room, telling them that we had an emergency but that it was probably over. Even so, they should be aware of it in the now unlikely case that there was a hidden fire and we would need to evacuate.

You don't tell a small town volunteer fire department that "There's a fire at the inn" and then expect them to calm down when you call back and tell them not to worry. When the FD came rushing through the dining room in full regalia complete with fire axes, they must have been surprised when the guests hardly looked up from their pancakes. One guest asked Ann, "Aren't they a tad overdressed?" I'm sure that the firefighters had expected, shall we say, a warmer reception. Our composed attitude was so calm that none of our guests was the least bit concerned. We were lucky that we never had to move to panic mode!

Brother, Can You Spare a Crapper?

It was a less than Merry Christmas morning when one of our toilets actually *broke*. I mean this in the literal sense, where the bowl cracked down the side and would not hold water. The timing was incredibly bad as the stores were closed and we were expecting a full house to check-in that night.

In a stroke of luck that I think can only happen in frugal New England, Liza, our favorite neighbor and muffin maker, just happened to have an "extra commode" gathering dust in her basement. It was an ugly green color, but that day it was the most beautiful thing in the world when I bolted it to the floor minutes before the next guest arrived.

But Seriously, Folks

Sometimes you can get caught up so much in your innkeeping that it feels like you have to put real life on hold until you can get back to it later. We missed just about every family gathering for fifteen years because they were scheduled during innkeeping times. But sadly, every once in a while something even worse than missed memories comes along.

In our first year of innkeeping, we had a very tragic experience. It was a winter evening and there were about twelve of us in the pub, sitting around the fireplace and chatting amiably after a tasty meatloaf dinner. The music was peaceful and the beer was delicious. It was near the end of the evening, and the fire was getting low. I asked if everybody was thinking of going to bed, or should we "commit to another log?" Everybody agreed that we wanted to keep going, and one guest volunteered to go outside to grab a log.

He came back to the group, log in hand, and plunked it onto the glowing coals in a cheery cascade of sparks. Then he crumpled to the ground with what was later determined to be a brain aneurysm.

Visiting fraternity brother Alan and I administered CPR for about a half an hour until the "Fast Squad" arrived. (In rural Vermont the name Fast Squad is more hopeful than descriptive.) The guest was 29 years old when he passed away that night and I was 29 years old when I watched him go. Ann stayed up all night with the widow waiting for her parents to get to the inn. It was an incredibly helpless feeling, and it was a lesson that carried us through the more difficult times. Not to sound trite, but no matter how difficult your situation is, it could be worse. We need to treasure every day because you never know when it will be your last.

The local newspaper ran the story with the headline "Skier Dies at Dinner," which wasn't entirely accurate. Nevertheless, we didn't serve meatloaf again that winter.

Now *That's* Dedication

There is another incredible story from our association that I would not believe unless I knew the innkeepers personally. I won't go into too many details, but the short of it is the husband (whose health was failing and whose inn was on the market for that reason) passed away just before breakfast. Mrs. Innkeeper kissed him on the forehead and went out to serve breakfast to the dozen unsuspecting guests.

She checked them out, waved goodbye and then when all the business was completed, *finally* called the coroner. Unless you are an innkeeper or an actor, you really can't appreciate just how much *"the show must go on"* attitude permeates your DNA.

I'm sure her husband would have understood completely.

Holy Belfry, Batman

The chambermaid was on the third floor when we heard her piercing scream all the way down in the kitchen. We ran upstairs with hearts aflutter. Our chambermaid was pointing and whimpering at four little legs hanging below a picture hung in the hallway.

Oh good grief, it was just two bats (love bats?) looking for a peaceful place to sleep the day away. The critters may scare mortal men (and chambermaids) but Vermont innkeepers are made of sterner stuff. All it takes is a big red Solo cup to pin them to the wall and a thin piece of cardboard to slide between the wall and the cup, trapping the little creatures inside the cup. Walk leisurely to the door and fling them to freedom. Then go throw cold water on the chambermaid and tell her to get back to work.

Deer Rampage

We were asleep when the crash happened. It was about 3 o'clock in the morning when we heard the disturbance in the back hall. Our first thought was that we had some after-hours revelers in the hot tub, but it soon became clear that even the most boisterous guest couldn't be making this much of a racket. There was such a commotion that Ann and I both decided to go see what was happening. Brandy, our aging yellow Labrador retriever, for once decided that this might be more interesting than a nap, so she padded along behind us as we made our little parade out of the owners quarters.

I opened the door to a scene out of a horror movie. A deer had jumped inside through a back window cutting itself on the foreleg in the process. The hallway was rather narrow, so I asked Ann to give me some room to see what I could do. Brandy was having none of this, and trotted back to bed. Go figure, I thought the dog would have gone nuts. I guess by now she was an innkeeper too and had seen it all.

If they ever do a _Bambi Meets the Texas Chainsaw Massacre_ movie, I can help them with the set design. First, make sure that the walls are covered in very expensive woven grass textured wallpaper. This makes for particularly attractive blood spatter as the freaked out deer bounds around like a drunken kangaroo. Then, have the deer leap repeatedly into a supply closet in a frightened effort to escape. Seven or eight jumps are really all it takes to splatter the entire inventory.

But then an amazing thing happened, and to this day I can hardly believe it. The deer was facing away from me, still leaping into the closet when I approached. I started talking soothingly, and it turned around and regarded me with a quizzical eye as if to ask, "Did you jump through that damn window, too?" I explained that no, I live here, but if she would like I could direct her to the nearest exit.

In the film *Finding Nemo*, Dory (Ellen DeGeneres) can "speak whale," and I apparently can "speak deer" because it turned around out of the closet and followed me down the hallway. I led it ever so peacefully around the corner and out the back door. It never said "thank you," though it didn't have to because I knew what it was thinking, for I am the deer whisperer.

One Last Shaggy Dog Story

We stopped putting mints on the pillows after about a year. It wasn't a cost-cutting measure as much as it was a strategic necessity after our Labrador retriever discovered, *"Hey, the food people also put mints on the bedroom pillows!"* After a while, it was just too embarrassing showing guests to their rooms, which were pristine except for the chewed up mint wrapper on the bed.

Final Thoughts

We hope that you have enjoyed learning a little about life behind the scenes at a country inn. Now get out there and go visit one - there is an innkeeper somewhere who could really use a hug.

And whatever you do, don't ever buy an inn.

Unless you're half-crazy.

Then it's okay.

The End

Addendum 1 – Don't Quit

When things go wrong, as they sometimes will,
When the road you're trudging seems all uphill,
When the funds are low and the debts are high,
And you want to smile, but you have to sigh,
When care is pressing you down a bit,
Rest, if you must, but don't you quit.

Life is queer with its twists and turns,
As every one of us sometimes learns,
And many a failure turns about,
When he might have won had he stuck it out;
Don't give up though the pace seems slow -
You may succeed with another blow.

Often the goal is nearer than,
It seems to a faint and faltering man,
Often the struggler has given up,
When he might have captured the victor's cup,
And he learned too late when the night came down,
How close he was to the golden crown.

Success is failure turned inside out –
The silver tint of the clouds of doubt,
And you never can tell how close you are,
It may be near when it seems so far,
So stick to the fight when you're hardest hit –
It's when things seem worst that you mustn't quit.

-Author unknown

Addendum 2 – TOP 10 LISTS from the last millennium

These TOP 10 LISTS are from our old webpage in the 1990's.

You may need to use a time machine to understand some of the humor!

They told the prospective guest that we don't take ourselves too seriously, and that there might be some fun to be had at our inn.

TOP 10 BEST Things about Innkeeping

10. Nice notes and gifts from guests.

9. Well-rounded, practical education, learning everything from wine, computers, plumbing, cooking and concrete to decorating, marketing and accounting.

8. Travel extensively for long periods in off seasons.

7. Reciprocal free country inn vacations.

6. Great wine cellar.

5. It's never boring.

4. Devour best seller list; time for continuing education classes, too!

3. Great tax deductions – like a nice stereo system and eclectic CD collection.

2. As the lead dog, the view never changes (and there is no such thing as office politics!)

1. Spend *real* quality time with family

TOP 10 WORST Things about Innkeeping

10. As in farming, the weather influences business greatly. Come on snow!

9. Sometimes too pooped to really enjoy the guests.

8. Most holidays reserved for guests, not family. (Ever try kicking out mom for Christmas?)

7. Long hours. Not really hard work, just long work.

6. Dishpan hands when the dishwasher breaks!

5. Cleaning the bathrooms when the chamber staff calls in sick.

4. The proverbial middle of the night guest request. (Only happened once in 12 years, but the potential always seems to be there)

3. Guests that don't show. Very rare, but a pain.

2. Plumbing.

1. Businesses pay more for everything. Mortgage interest, electricity, commercial equipment etc.

TOP 10 BEST Pieces of Advice for Prospective Innkeepers

10. Never start an inn from scratch, but invest in a solid reputation.

9. Get flu shots each year.

8. Get competitive quotes - from insurance, mortgage, credit cards, and wood, to chimney sweeps.

7. Invest in an answering machine and two expensive vacuums.

6. Take a forced day off and regular rejuvenation vacations (even if you think you don't need them).

5. Pay top dollar for good, dependable staff.

4. Rent your linens.

3. Be handy or willing to learn.

2. Never lose your sense of humor. The inn is an incredible source of fun if you let it and look for it!

1. Just do it!

TOP 10 BEST things about being Salt Ash Innkeepers

10. Salt Ash babies - 7 and counting!

9. Salt Ash engagements – 4 so far (and 2 weddings)

8. New septic system.

7. Fifteen weeks' vacation.

6. No more projects!

5. Glen's golf handicap fell from 14 to 4 (okay, and back up again)

4. No commute, zero traffic!

3. We get to live in Vermont!

2. TV in kitchen - cook to Olympics, presidential debates, Thursday lineup.

1. Free Killington ski passes.

TOP 10 WORST things about being Salt Ash Innkeepers

This one was particularly hard to develop because there are so darn many. To share the pain, we decided to put this one to music. By now you're probably sick of songs set to the 12 days of Christmas, so suffer along as we have for the past 12 years...

12 chambermaids
11 no longer working
10 septic pump outs
9 broken windows
8 forgot room keys
7 regurgitation's...
6 by the dog
5 brand new roofs
4 long distance carriers
3 dishwashers
2 ice machines
And a ju-u-ury of our peers!

TOP 10 BEST Reasons to Visit the Salt Ash Inn

10. OJ doesn't ski.

9. Deer season is over and venison is cheap.

8. Beavis and Butthead don't ski (heh. heh-heh) but Ren and Stimpy do (Joy!)

7. You won't see Rush Limbaugh in hot pink spandex racing gear.

6. Vermont's still a safe haven to wear your fur coat.

5. Easy commute to breakfast.

4. 9,609 incredibly beautiful square miles and no billboards.

3. Every Vermont snowflake is different.

2. PC just a means Plymouth Cheese.

1. Two words: Damn Quaint.

TOP 10 BEST Reasons to Give a Salt Ash Inn Gift Certificate

10. Avoid embarrassing size questions at Frederick's of Hollywood

9. Easier to gift wrap than a Corvette.

8. Gift certificates are printed with soy ink and are recyclable.

7. Leona Helmsley cleans our toilets.

6. You won't see Ross Perot in hot pink spandex racing gear.

5. Dick Vitale no longer broadcasts Killington ski reports.

4. Like a fine wine, they appreciate with age.

3. Buy enough, and you can make an Oscar dress out of them.

2. Chunky Monkey doesn't mail well

1. After $100 million in gift certificates, God will call Oral Roberts home.

TOP 10 Salt Ash Inn Stupid Pet Tricks

Okay, so they're not all pets, but these animal adventures really happened at the Salt Ash Inn

10. Our old dog Brandy munches porcupine, gets vicious case of quill mouth.

9. Deer jumps through window into the inn.

8. Guest unearths worm farm in fresh corn on the cob.

7. Homeless raccoon family takes up residence in dumpster

6. Skunk takes whirlwind tour through basement.

5. Stowaway cat in guest luggage.

4. Brandy catches vacationing cockatiel (and returns it safely).

3. Visiting dog pees on (our old) couch.

2. Bat family invades fireplace. Holy smokes!

1. Turn down service fails - Brandy eats mints off all the pillows.

TOP 10 Salt Ash Inn Stupid Guest Tricks

Yes indeed, not all guests are perfect. Below are some of the reasons that we tell prospective innkeepers that the most important requirement of being an innkeeper is having an open mind and a sense of humor.

10. Flushed a night light (required taking apart toilet).

9. Wringing green Play-Doh through antique clothes ringer.

8. Diabetic leaves half dozen used needles stuck in wall.

7. Turning brochures upside down (played out!)

6. X-rated hot tubbers (yes, you guessed it…)

5. High school kids hide Boones Farm in toilet tank (like we wouldn't find it!)

4. Bachelorettes leave stuffed animals hanging from ceiling fan.

3. Setting alarm clocks under each other's beds.

2. Smoking in non-smoking rooms and thinking everyone else's sense of smell is broken…

1. Guest hides money under plastic bag in wastebasket, and then forgets where he put it.

TOP 10 Answers to Salt Ash Inn
Frequently Asked Questions

10. Yes, it's real Vermont maple syrup.

9. No, that was Woodstock, New York.

8. Glen went to Washington and Lee and worked in the insurance world.

7. Ann went to Harvard and worked as a computer techie nerd.

6. Bob Newhart is our idol, and Darryl and Darryl are not here.

5. Ann and Glen liked visiting inns, wanted to work for themselves, and chose to spend every blinking moment of their married lives together.

4. Saltash was the original name of the town of Plymouth. There is still a town of Saltash next to the town of Plymouth in England

3. The inn was built in 1830 as a stagecoach stop, general store, and blacksmith shop. It was also used as the town dance hall and post office.

2. Dominos does not deliver, and it takes 25 minutes to get to McDonald's.

1. The first $1.2 million takes it.

Read a brief excerpt from
How I Wrote 2 eBooks in 21 Days

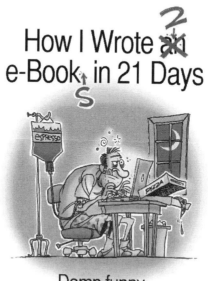

How I Wrote a 2 e-Book s in 21 Days

Damn funny.
Seriously.

By Glen Stanford

What's it like to write your first e-book? Is it difficult? Can I do it? Why is there air?

These are all good questions, and I'll tackle most of them here.

We have air because the gravitational pull of the earth holds the oxygen molecules close to the ground into what we have labeled an "atmosphere."

In other words, the earth sucks.

I'm really hoping that my book won't.

I read Steve Scott's *How to Write a Nonfiction eBook in 21 days*, and it got me enthused enough to write the "how to make money in innkeeping" book that has been bottled up inside of me for two decades. I did indeed make Steve's deadline, and completed both *this book* and *THE BREAD IS IN THE BED* exactly 21 days after I put the first note on the first index card.

The day after I decided to write BREAD BED, I thought it might be fun to take notes on the experience. Hey, I'm a rookie; this is my first book. Someday I may want to reminisce about the start of my glory years.

By the end of the third day, I had decided to write *TWO* e-books in 21 days. (Every guy knows that *more is always better*; it's a Y-chromosome thing.) One e-book would be the book about innkeeping, and the second would be *the book about writing the book* about innkeeping. Never one to do things by halves, I have a tendency to bite off more than I can chew (though I will never admit that to my wife).

For example, my lovely bride (everybody say "hi" to Ann. "*Hi, Ann.*") wanted to go sailing, so I signed us up for a 1,500 mile/11 day offshore crewing "opportunity" on a 40ft sailboat traveling from Virginia to the British Virgin Islands. She thought we could use a little exercise, so I arranged for us to hike 650 miles on the Appalachian Trail. She said that I could indulge my whim to look into beekeeping, so I bought *sixteen hives*. You're beginning to get the idea, right? Welcome to my wife's Hell.

The week of January 27 started out much like every other week here in sunny Florida. The skies were clear, the temperature was in the mid-70s; in short: a lot of the "what's not to like" department. That is, until I had the brainstorm to write an e-book. So: sunny outside, brainstorm inside. Are you with me so far? Try to keep up.

"Just do it" the Nike commercials keep telling me. So on that delightfully sunny afternoon on what will hereinafter ever be known as DAY ONE, Monday, January 28, 2013, a day that will most likely not live in too much infamy, I finished Steve's how-to book and decided "Why the heck not?" Pretty inspiring, right?

It was Steve's book that was the last straw on the camel's back (when was the last time you saw a straw laden camel?) It fired-up the final neuron in my brain that said "*You've been gabbing about writing this book for twenty years, and it's about time you got off your fat ass and wrote that book; or more to the point, set your fat ass down on a chair and wrote that book.*" It was a pretty big neuron.

This book is the companion piece to *THE BREAD IS IN THE BED* – a "making-of story" much in the same vein as the making of *Star Wars* films. But with fewer Wookies. It's a behind the scenes look at an exinnkeeper/ ex-Appalachian Trail hiker /ex-New England Patriots cheerleader/ would-be author and current yacht captain as I try to follow the plan in Steve's book to produce my e-book(s) in 21 days. What makes this book extraordinary is that it is jam-packed with *dozens* of attempts at humor!

It is "blog-like," although the final product is cleaned up and the swear words are edited. I take to heart author John Locke's excellent advice in *How I Sold 1 Million eBooks in 5 Months*. He says that your e-book (and I'm paraphrasing here) can pretty much suck as long as you sell it cheap and a few people like it.

In other words, to be successful with an e-book, you need to find a loyal group of people who enjoy your writing style and would consume anything that you publish. Well, since I devour everything Mr. Locke writes, I can certainly buy into that approach! Plus, he was kind enough to put his picture on the cover so I know when not to open the door.

So, I'm trying to write a whimsical book (make that *TWO* books) with my sense of humor. Not everyone will think that they are knee-slappers, but with any luck there are folks out there who would enjoy them enough to consider telling a friend to *read this dude*. That's me. The dude. Pretty hip, right?

Made in the USA
Middletown, DE
31 October 2014